Federalism and Free Trade

JEAN-LUC MIGUÉ

*École Nationale d'Administration Publique,
University of Quebec*

IEA

Published by

INSTITUTE OF ECONOMIC AFFAIRS

1993

First published in May 1993

by

THE INSTITUTE OF ECONOMIC AFFAIRS

2 Lord North Street, Westminster,
London SW1P 3LB

Hobart Paper 122

The Institute gratefully acknowledges financial support for its publications programme and other work from a generous benefaction by the late Alec and Beryl Warren.

Printed in Great Britain by

GORON PRO-PRINT CO LTD

6 Marlborough Road, Churchill Industrial Estate, Lancing, W. Sussex

Text set in Berthold Baskerville

CONTENTS

[3]

FOREWORD

The debate in Britain about 'Europe' is polarised. Positions have been taken up on both sides and are being defended, often on largely emotional grounds. Some issues, such as European monetary arrangements, have been examined by economists. But surprisingly little economic analysis has been applied to the wider issues which are raised by Britain's membership of the Community and especially by the proposed ratification of the Maastricht Treaty. Particularly important is the question of the costs and benefits of the move to extend the European Community well beyond a free trade region towards a union in which there are centrally determined policies for many aspects of economic and social affairs. It is this gap which is filled by Professor Migué's careful analysis in this *Hobart Paper* (No. 122) which, in a wide-ranging and original examination of the relationship between federalism and free trade, throws light on many issues of concern to those who watch the formation of trading blocs and are worried that those blocs may become inward-looking.

Migué begins (in Section II) by pointing out that, among all the policy instruments which governments employ, '. . . protectionism stands out as radically different from all others' (page 14) because it removes the constraint which free trade places on what would otherwise be government monopoly power. A government which wishes to pursue wealth-redistributing policies can do so only if it erects barriers to trade. If there is free trade, increases in taxes and stricter regulation in pursuit of such policies will bring about substitution of overseas goods and services for local production; capital and labour will also 'vote with their feet' by moving abroad. Thus a government which wishes to pursue redistributive policies is constrained by the knowledge that its own citizens must bear the full costs of those policies. Free trade therefore '. . . contributes to solving the problem of the monopolistic state by limiting the power of government' (page 15).

Canadian experience is used by Migué to illustrate some of the problems which arise when governments of federal states or of common markets try to avoid the consequences of free trade. He argues that

> 'The lion's share of federal budgets and regulations in Canada is used to shelter provinces from the consequences of their own decisions ... the more inefficient a province is, the more it is compensated by central hand-outs' (page 18).

Migué contends that '. . . the Maastricht Treaty implies a similar transfer mechanism in Europe' (page 18). Ireland, for example, which stands to collect large sums in adjustment payments to close the 'prosperity gap', was 'literally bought'. But the effect of such hand-outs is to increase regional disparities by discouraging resources from moving to their most productive locations, as well as making the Community less competitive *vis-à-vis* the rest of the world. Moreover, according to Migué, free trade is a very important constraint on the '. . . tax appetite of the Leviathan' (page 25) because it implies that taxes on resources must be compensated by equivalent benefits for resource owners.

In the debate about Europe, 'federalism' is often equated with centralisation. Professor Migué takes the opposite view. True federalism occurs when '. . . most responsibilities are entrusted to decentralised authorities which have no power to tax or regulate the whole area where trade is free' (page 27). Free trade is thus essentially a federalising process: where it exists, decisions are automatically decentralised and a smaller share of resources is transferred to governments because citizens can avoid measures which they do not want. In a free trade, federalist community even the provision of so-called 'public goods' should be more efficiently achieved in smaller groups with similar tastes since one of the factors determining where people choose to live will be the public services which are provided.

Professor Migué also provides (in Section IV) a fascinating analysis of the tendency towards centralisation in the European Community which results in a stream of policy proposals from the centre—whether in social affairs, transport, technology, training, energy or 'industrial policy'. As he explains, 'balkanisation' by centralisation is predictable. Member-states of a common market are unable, because of free trade, to shift the burden of their own costly policies to other members. But the central authority faces no such constraints because that burden can be shifted to outsiders. It constantly produces redistributive policies, driven by the self-interest of the central bureaucracy, pressure

[8]

from producer groups (which concentrate their lobbying on the centre), and pressure also from less-developed members of the common market which stand to gain from such policies. There is a tendency towards service uniformity and imposed harmonisation (rather than the 'natural' harmonisation which free trade engenders). Even as trade barriers among members are apparently reduced, the community is balkanised by central policies which subsidise some and tax others, dissociating regional costs from regional prices and erecting fresh barriers to trade.

Despite Professor Migué's concern about present directions in Europe, the advantages of federalism and free trade persuade him that the

'... combination of a single market with decentralised national governments can work for the general welfare, because it is based on competitive principles ... The virtue of free trade is to transfer control over wealth from governments to individuals' (page 69).

Free trade will increase wealth and reduce government's ability to indulge in transfers using other people's money. It will diminish the influence of organised interest groups which will find rent-seeking less profitable. But to gain these advantages, trade must indeed be freed. The centralising tendencies of the authorities in Brussels (and corresponding authorities elsewhere) which substitute new barriers for old, must be curbed. Then '... federalism and free trade should strengthen governments' power to do good, while restricting their power to abuse citizens' (page 70).

The views expressed in this *Hobart Paper* are those of the author, not of the Institute (which has no corporate view), its Trustees, Directors or Advisers. Professor Migué's powerful and persuasive exposition of the advantages of free trade and his criticisms of centralising tendencies in Europe and elsewhere are published as a contribution to discussion, particularly about the direction in which the European Community is proceeding.

May 1993   COLIN ROBINSON
Editorial Director, Institute of Economic Affairs;
Professor of Economics, University of Surrey

THE AUTHOR

JEAN-LUC MIGUÉ is Professor of Economics at the School of Public Administration of the University of Quebec, in Quebec City. He graduated from the University of Montreal, pursued post-graduate studies at the London School of Economics in the 1950s, and received his PhD from the American University, Washington, DC. He specialises in the application of economic methods to government choices. He has written extensively on various issues of applied economic theory and policy. He has served as a member of task forces and as consultant for a number of organisations active in education, the environment and telecommunications. His current research interests include the selection of policy instruments, the economics of property rights as applied to environmental policies, and federalism.

Professor Migué's publications include *The Price of Health* (1974), *Nationalistic Policies in Canada: An Economic Approach* (1979), *L'économiste et la chose publique* (1979), and *Le monopole public de l'éducation* (1989). He has contributed articles to many journals, including *The Canadian Journal of Economics*, *The Cato Journal*, *The Journal of Law and Economics*, *La Revue économique*, *Public Choice*, *La Revue française de finances publiques*, *Hacienda Publica Espanola*, etc. He is a Fellow of the Royal Society of Canada.

I. INTRODUCTION

'A modern economy is the most effectual bridle ever invented against the folly of despotism.'

Sir James Steuart, *An Inquiry into the Principles of Political Oeconomy*, 1767.

As the world moves toward freer trade, both within the trading blocs which are emerging and among nations in general, national state monopolies no longer seem profitable, the political and military gains associated with nation-states recede and the benefits of acceding to vast markets increase. Protectionism is less and less a viable instrument of intervention by national governments. The purpose of this *Hobart Paper* is to assess the implications of such world trends for the policies of national and local governments.

It is argued that, provided there is free inward and outward movement of factors and goods, a national government has little power to engage in redistributive policies. Stated conversely, it is the ability to restrict international movements of factors and goods which enables government to engage in costly redistributive policies. The member-governments of a common market are in a position approximating that of the government of a small economy. Decentralised *federalism** and free trade are desirable inasmuch as they strengthen governments' power to do good, while restricting their power to abuse citizens.

The paper, which is cast in terms of choice of policy instruments, provides a formal framework for analysing the effect on domestic policies of constraining the power of national governments to maintain trade barriers, for instance by GATT-type arrangements, common-market treaties and other freer-trade agreements within trading blocs. It shows that opening national frontiers to freer movement of goods, services, capital and people results in less use of interventionist instruments in domestic affairs.

---

*Words and phrases set in italics and followed by an asterisk are defined/explained in the 'Glossary', below, pp. 71-74.

Less reliance on protectionism by a national government has an impact similar to devolution of power within a federal state. Without the power to close their borders to goods and services, to capital and to people, national and regional governments discover that resort to domestic policy instruments like spending, taxes and regulations for redistributive purposes is more costly, indeed impossible. Heavy taxes and restrictive regulations on national resources in conditions of free trade lead to more rapid, more pronounced substitution of foreign for local production. They also cause capital to move out of higher-cost economies. Moreover, victims of government abuse may 'vote with their feet' and leave the territory.

Free Trade Equals Federalisation

Freer trade places national and regional governments in a similar position to that of a decentralised government in a traditional federal state. In effect, free trade is a sufficient condition for the federalisation of the world. The mobility (exit) of goods and people acts as an alternative to politics (voice) as a process for revealing preferences in matters of public goods. Under true federalism, resource owners can choose the administration in which they place their assets.

This competitive federalist model can work only if national and local decisions are not over-ruled by central powers within trade blocs or at supra-national level. As a tool for cartelising national and regional governments, *centralisation** (defined as the ability to rule over an entire common market) weakens the ability of citizens to escape unpopular measures by moving their goods or their productive factors to more favourable locations and uses.

Section II presents the choice of policy instruments, when there are external constraints on trade barriers and the mobility of resources among members of a federalist governmental structure limits the ability of local and national governments to resort to domestic policy tools. General implications of federalism at the common market level are derived in Section III. Centralisation is shown in Section IV to imply the *balkanisation** of common markets and to run counter both to efficiency requirements and to the logic of federalism. In Section V, broad historical trends in the size of the public economy and the extent of protectionism are shown to be consistent with the paper's thesis. Section VI derives constitutional principles which follow from the earlier analysis.

[12]

II. PROTECTIONISM AS A PREREQUISITE
TO OTHER POLICY INSTRUMENTS

The Theoretical Underpinnings

Analysis of the impact of trade-barrier constraints on domestic policies of national governments must start from a theory of the choice of instruments by governments and, in particular, from recent literature,[1] which argues that policy instruments are substitutes for one another.[2] The prevailing opinion is that redistributive and other political objectives can be more fully achieved by resort to more than a single instrument. As one policy choice (say, government spending) is subjected to institutional constraints, it is assumed that legislators will resort to other instruments (say, regulation). For example, as budgetary limits and treaty provisions prevent politicians from indulging further in the subsidisation of farmers, supply management of farm production can be substituted. Coercive provision of day-care services by employers can be substituted for family allowances and provision by monopoly state suppliers. Mandatory health services imposed on employers can be substituted for public medicare with similar redistributive results.

Some analysts are therefore unenthusiastic about the idea of imposing constitutional or legal limits on the power of legislators to tax, to spend and to regulate. A paper by Hahn, for example, states quite explicitly:

> 'Suppose . . . that Congress chooses to limit spending. Assuming that spending was a more efficient instrument for transferring wealth at the margin leads to the conclusion that government must extract more resources from the economy. Thus, the economy shrinks and government grows.'[3]

Once it is accepted that policy instruments are substitutes for one another, this conclusion follows.

---

[1] Robert W. Hahn, 'Instrument Choice, Political Reform and Economic Welfare', *Public Choice*, Vol. 67, December 1990, pp. 243-56.

[2] A more technical discussion of this question is offered in J.-L. Migué, 'Trade Barriers in the Theory of Instrument Choice', *The Cato Journal*, Vol. 12, Fall 1992.

[3] Hahn, *op. cit.*, p. 249.

However, this model has to be modified fundamentally when assessing the impact of trade-barrier limits on other policy tools because, in the arsenal of redistributive instruments available to governments, protectionism stands out as radically different from all others. Most domestic policy instruments are complementary to, rather than substitutes for, protectionism in the pursuit of political goals. More specifically, as a tool to redistribute wealth among various groups, trade barriers are a prerequisite to the use of all others. As exogenous constraints are applied on the use of tariff or non-tariff barriers, local and national legislators must reduce rather than increase resort to other instruments. That is why members of a traditional federal state or of a common market cannot transfer the burden of local policies to outside producers and consumers.

Residents in a relatively small-size economy bear the burden of inefficient government policies just as they benefit from efficient policies. The reason is that the prices of goods and services, capital and labour are determined outside those economies. Neither the province within a federal state nor the national government within a common market is in a position to influence prices outside their borders. National economies are more open than the common market economy of which they are members and thus are more subject to competition from non-local suppliers of goods, capital and labour.

Even under a protectionist régime, prices are determined on world markets. However, there is one basic difference under freer trade. The free movement of resources means that any domestic measure which reduces efficiency and is implemented by a national government imposes a heavier burden on the residents. Opening the economy to freer trade increases the local elasticity of supply because it allows producers and consumers to shift their resources and their sources of supply.

Freer Trade Protects Consumers

Granted that local and national governments have no power to influence prices outside their territories, it follows that the removal of trade barriers substantially increases the burden of internal policies. Domestic interventions are made more costly to local residents. Imposing significantly heavier taxes and stricter regulations increases relative production costs and, under free trade, causes a more rapid and more pronounced substitution of imported goods and services for local production.

[14]

Consumers are in this way protected from successful lobbying of national authorities by producer interests. Moreover, factor owners can move their capital to neighbouring jurisdictions and, at the limit, 'vote with their feet' by leaving the territory. Because inefficient government decisions cost more the more open the economy, less interventionism is to be expected.

Put differently, domestic interventions exert their influence through changes they bring about in the relative prices of goods, capital and labour within the national territory. Because local economies are price takers rather than price makers, the only way for national legislators to have some lasting impact on prices internally is to maintain trade barriers. Without the power to close their borders to foreign competition, national governments discover that most other tools formally available to them to pursue political objectives are of little value, because resort to such instruments becomes too costly.

Free trade therefore contributes to solving the problem of the monopolistic state by limiting the power of government. Because of competition from governments outside the regional or national territory, freer trade limits the power already divided among national authorities and prevents them from imposing taxes and regulations the population does not want. A de-centralised governmental régime enables the population of a common market to move their goods, their capital and/or themselves away from national tax and regulatory measures that are detrimental to them. In that sense it offers citizens an additional instrument to discipline governments. To analysts of anti-trust policy, the analogue with the market power of business firms should be obvious. Just as trade can perform the function of anti-trust policy in constraining market power, so can it act as a curb on government power.[4]

Practical Illustrations

Some examples of the effects of freer trade follow.

Restrictive Labour Laws

Under the post-1992 European Community free-trade system, affirmative-action measures (part of the so-called Social Charter) and restrictive labour laws in some European nations will result in more significant drops in income and employment than under the previous régime. Artificially increased labour costs in the

[4] I am grateful to an anonymous referee for suggesting this parallel.

most rigidly regulated countries will depress output more significantly and repel investment. It is already obvious that with the price of labour the highest in the world at $25 an hour, labour costs in Germany represent a growing drag on the economy and that 'foreign lands' are more attractive to capital. France has similar problems. Following Hoover's decision to switch vacuum cleaner production from Dijon to Scotland, an indignant Prime Minister of France condemned such 'social dumping' practices on the part of business firms in search of 'lower terms'.

It is not surprising that there is a centralist movement in favour of a pan-European social charter. After the advent of free trade, national 'industrial policies' of European governments will place a heavier burden than before on domestic producers, since tax-financed aid to selected 'winners' and inefficient sectors will lead to increased substitution of imports. Prosperous companies and workers in France and Belgium will find it more burdensome, for instance, to underwrite national airlines which ask for subsidies. Producers in prosperous regions will find it harder to support the cost of development aid to depressed areas of the national economy. In maintaining high-cost regulated telecommunications suppliers and securities exchanges, national regulators will impose a heavier burden on the purchasers of their expensive services after 1992. Their ability to compete in the more open field of Europe will become more difficult with the common market in place.

Rail and Postal Services

Having to purchase rail and postal services from high-cost national monopolies will make life more difficult for national firms as they face the more competitive environment of post-1992 Europe. Free trade is what brings the European Commission to propose throwing member-countries' mail services into competition with one another. Great Britain's proposed privatisation of its mail services is seen by some as a way to lure European bulk users to its shores.

Agriculture

Nothing in the free-trade agreement between Canada and the USA prohibits the political manipulation of agricultural supply. Nevertheless, the value of milk quotas has already dropped in Canada since the signing of the accord. Pressure by food processors to have quotas removed is intensifying. To understand better the situation of Canadian food processors and farmers after the free-trade deal with the United States, imagine that no Common Agricultural Policy is in place in Europe. Instead, agricultural price support and output control are left to national governments, while processed food producers compete in a single market and remain free to buy their supplies from the cheapest sources.

Financial Markets

Competition from foreign financial markets, as much as from domestic participants, is forcing US legislators to loosen constraints on financial institutions. Public companies in the USA are subject to the world's strictest disclosure and insider trading rules. But, if it can be shown that foreign rules protect investors equally as well as US rules, the US regulatory system will come under pressure to change. Such pressures already exist as foreign companies refuse to list on the Big Board,[5] because they do not want to abide by US disclosure requirements. Similarly, high rates of return on capital in newly capitalist economies such as India, Mexico, Chile, and so on, act as a brake on US redistributionists who wish to increase top marginal income tax rates. Competitive pressures such as these originate from the ease with which funds can be moved across national borders and evade national protectionist controls.

Monetary Arrangements

The debate on monetary arrangements in Europe can also be seen against this analytical background. The conventional view is that moving to a full currency union on the lines of the Maastricht Treaty is the way to achieve greater economic stability: only inter-regional fiscal transfers, possible under centralised currency régimes, can guarantee a workable, stable system. This conclusion is not only disturbing, it is incorrect.

Full monetary integration, whether inside single countries or in Europe, does not suppress the cost of inconsistent regional or national policies. A currency union merely shifts the cost of adjustment to the more prosperous regions of the union. The Maritime provinces (declining regions) can pursue costly policies within the Canadian currency union because they are subsidised to the tune of billions of dollars for their failure to

5 In the language of Wall Street, 'Big Board' means the New York Stock Exchange.

[17]

'adjust'. Downward pressure exerted on the Canadian dollar by secessionist threats reduces the living standards of all Canadians, not merely of Quebeckers, as a result of deteriorating terms of trade and higher interest rates. In both cases the adjustment cost is merely shifted to other Canadian provinces by the action of the central monopoly.

The Canadian Example: Economic Absurdity

In Canada, shared-cost programmes, equalisation and regional policies, the central provision of local services as well as the extension nationally of provincial regulations (for example, in agriculture, transportation, telecommunications and fisheries) serve to sterilise the local economic costs implied by provincial policies, neutralising the federalist adjustment process. The lion's share of federal budgets and regulations in Canada is used to shelter provinces from the consequences of their own decisions. They act as implicit regional tariffs, regional quotas or discriminatory subsidies to regional consumers and producers. The more inefficient a province is, the more it is compensated by central hand-outs. 'Adjustment' as understood under the Canadian currency union is an exercise in economic absurdity.

Maastricht: Moving the Canadian Way?

It is now clear that the Maastricht treaty implies a similar transfer mechanism in Europe. The Irish referendum on Maastricht was fought almost entirely on that ground. The Irish were literally bought. Ireland stands to collect $12 billion-worth of aid and special benefits from the European commitment to close 'the prosperity gap'. To designate such practices as 'adjustment' is clearly a misuse of language. Under real-world currency union régimes, instability is not removed. It is subsumed under the false equilibrium of political hand-outs. In the long run, interregional disparities in income growth are amplified, as resources are discouraged from moving to their most productive locations.

The Alternative of Currency Competition

What is the alternative? What are the policy and institutional implications of this vision for Europe and North America? The régime most likely to deliver stability, combined with national responsibility and freedom from coercive transfers by supranational authority, is currency competition. Freely floating currencies circulating together in a common market, with or

[18]

without an ERM-style mechanism, constitute competitive federalism applied to monetary matters. Individuals and businesses can hold assets in any currency they choose. There are then powerful incentives for national authorities to deliver the kind of performance people want. Irresponsible micro- and macro-economic policies cause dissatisfied individuals to switch to other currencies, as costly policies make the economy less competitive.

Because there is no way of knowing in advance the optimal size of a currency area, one can only rely on the market process of discovery to arrive at a determination. If the advantages of a single European or North American currency as a way of minimising transactions costs are so overwhelming, such a system will spontaneously evolve as the choice of Europeans and North Americans. In the meantime, free competition in currencies offers individuals protection against irresponsible national policies, sheltering prosperous countries from the dangers of a Eurofed and other institutionalised hand-outs to weak and inefficient regions.

The process by which discipline is imposed on national authorities under a system of multiple currencies is as follows. The mobility of capital and other resources within common markets penalises regions with riskier currencies which have higher interest rates and lower standards of living. Weak exchange rates rather than central hand-outs befall regions which lose investors' confidence as a result of costly policies. At the same time, such regions are enabled to compete by declines in their living standards coincident on deteriorating terms of trade, not shifts of the burden of their policies to other nationals via central hand-outs. Each nation assumes the burden of its choices. A single common market does not imply a common currency, any more than it calls for a common social policy or a common language. Europe would do well to emulate North America and turn its back on arrangements designed to encourage rent-seeking by national members.

Pegged-rate régimes give rise to recurrent ERM-style crises. The recent European monetary crisis is itself a signal to national governments that their micro- and macro-economic policies have been inconsistent with exchange rate stability. Either they adjust or they do not. In all circumstances they bear the cost of their decision. A common currency régime would in no way facilitate the adjustment and would not deliver the benefits of

[19]

greater economic stability. It would merely shift the adjustment cost from irresponsible and inefficient regions to those which are responsible and efficient.

Social planners have always held that planning under monopoly removes costly duplication associated with market competition. History and analysis teach an entirely different lesson. The centralist vision overestimates the potential benefits from centralised decision-making and underestimates the rewards from competition.

Resource Mobility and Taxes as Fees for Services

The single most convincing piece of evidence on the strength of resource mobility is the consistent convergence of *per capita* income across regions of the United States and across a broad sample of countries over past decades.[6] Convergence occurred in the past despite the numerous hurdles set up by governments against the movement of goods and factors between national communities. As barriers to trade are removed, tendencies towards income homogeneity between regions are reinforced.

The process of income convergence is important. It shows that resource owners in all regions respond to incentives by moving on the basis of compensations received, including regional taxes, regulations and services. Individuals have been shown to be sensitive to the combination of taxes and services offered at the regional level.[7] The rising tax burden is seen by R. Vedder as having increased taxpayers' sensitivity to local variations in tax loads.[8] Increased reliance on the pricing of public services in recent years is interpreted as a consequence of this higher awareness by taxpayers.

After three decades of debate about capital mobility as a constraint on arbitrary action by government, it is generally agreed that tax rate differentials are important determinants of location for business firms, within the USA and between the

[6] For a recent examination of this question, see R. J. Barro and X. Sala-i-Martin, 'Convergence', *Journal of Political Economy*, Vol. 100, April 1992, pp. 223-51, and W. J. Baumol *et al.*, *Productivity and American Leadership: The Long View*, Cambridge, Mass.: MIT Press, 1989.

[7] See R. J. Cebula, *The Determinants of Human Migrations*, Lexington, Mass.: Lexington Books, 1979, and R. J. Cebula and M. Z. Kafoglis, 'A Note on the Tiebout-Tullock Hypothesis: The Period 1975-80', *Public Choice*, Vol. 48, 1976, pp. 65-69.

[8] R. Vedder, 'Tiebout Taxes and Economic Growth', *The Cato Journal*, Vol. 10, Spring-Summer 1990, pp. 91-108.

USA and other nations.[9] Firms move their capital away from jurisdictions with heavier tax burdens by 'transfer pricing' (the price 'foreign' companies charge or pay for parts shipped to or from their own 'local' affiliates). In order to reduce reported earnings from plants located in a high-tax country, a foreign owner can overcharge for parts shipped to this local subsidiary. Viewed by local tax collectors as a threat to their tax base, such tax evasion works only because the foreign owner is based in a low-tax country. The practice is an important competitive weapon for investors to rein in the tax appetite of national governments in a freely trading world.

Local Property Taxes and Capital Migration

The debate about local property taxes as determinants of capital migration is also directly relevant to the analysis. Two authorities[10] concluded that real property taxes are distortionary taxes on capital, rather than benefit taxes related to individual consumption of local public goods such as education. Because local authorities in the United States find themselves unable to ensure that the last dollar paid in taxes equals the taxpayer's marginal willingness to pay for local services, wholesale *free-riding** is said to take place on local public goods. Large families can rent lots (plots) on the fringe of cities, park trailers on them and send their children to the local school at little cost to themselves. This result implies that owners of real property in the same neighbourhood are charged tax prices higher than the value of local benefits received, which tends to drive capital away. Undesirable distortions in the geographical allocation of capital are seen arising from this process.

In the latest examination of this question, however, it has been shown[11] that local zoning laws are effective in transforming property taxes into fees for local public services. Municipalities

9 L. B. Benson and R. N. Johnson, 'The Lagged Impact of State and Local Taxes on Economic Activity and Political Behavior', *Economic Enquiry*, Vol. 24, July 1986, pp. 389-401; J. R. Hines, Jr. and E. M. Rice, 'Fiscal Paradise: Foreign Tax Havens and American Business', NBER Working Paper No. 3477, October 1990; and D. Harris, R. Morck, J. B. Slemrod, and B. Yeung, 'Income Shifting in U.S. Multinational Corporations', NBER Working Paper No. 3924, December 1991.

10 P. Mieszkowski and G. R. Zodrow, 'The Incidence of the Property Tax: The Benefit View Versus the New View', in G. R. Zodrow (ed.), *Local Provision of Public Services*, New York: Academic Press, 1983, pp. 109-29.

11 W. A. Fischel, 'Property Taxation and the Tiebout Model : Evidence for the Benefit View from Zoning and Voting', *Journal of Economic Literature*, Vol. 30, March 1992, pp. 171-77.

do not explicitly exclude low-cost housing, because that would be struck down in the courts. Instead they use quantifiable rules such as minimum lot size to deter unwelcome developers and to minimise rent-seeking. Other exclusionary devices are also available: these include

> 'single-family use; one structure per lot; minimum lot size; maximum lot coverage; minimum floor area of the house; off-street parking; front, side and rear yard setbacks; maximum height restrictions; designation of costly-to-serve areas as agricultural, forestry, wetland, or otherwise off-limits',[12]

and other devices such as up-front impact fees to cover subsidised development of above-average public infrastructure. Fiscal zoning is the instrument used by local governments to make development pay its own way. Property taxation endures because fiscal zoning transforms it into a benefit tax, protected from wholesale free-riding and rent-seeking by residents. Reduced taxation of farmlands and reductions for elderly taxpayers are other examples of adjustments conceded by local officials to residents who do not impose heavy fiscal burdens.

Overcoming Rent-Seeking by Migration

Why do towns and cities strive to adjust dollars paid in taxes to the level of benefits received in local services and in so doing succeed in overcoming rent-seeking by migration? The answer is that they have little latitude to do otherwise. By virtue of the high mobility of resources between their territory and the outside world, tax and regulatory burdens not compensated by benefits in services develop into movements away from areas which impose them. Alternatively, should benefits exceed local taxes and regulatory costs, the likely inflow of people attracted by potential gains tends to dissipate the rent, which is also an unattractive prospect for current residents. In other words, distortionary taxes and regulations are extremely costly to local residents because of the high elasticity of supply of resources. Consequently, inefficient migrations into and out of local territories are unlikely to occur.

The ability of decentralised authorities to minimise rent-seeking by migrations is not limited to municipalities. There are real-world examples at provincial and even national levels. For instance, so that only its citizens would share in its oil rent, the

---

[12] *Ibid.*, p. 173.

state of Alaska originally limited the distribution of its tax take on oil to residents who were in the state before enactment of the measure: the scheme was rejected by the US Supreme Court. In the run up to the Chinese takeover of Hong Kong in 1997, Canada and other countries are offering wealthy Hong Kong residents the right of citizenship if they invest a minimum amount in the host economy. Gary Becker[13] has proposed to institutionalise a similar process by substituting an auction system for the arbitrary criteria now in place to select immigrants. Because of the relatively low mobility of its French-speaking population, the Canadian Province of Quebec has had to rely more than other provinces on payroll taxes than on profit taxes to finance its programmes. There are, of course, equity implications in many such alternatives. Nevertheless, economists of traditional persuasion who invoke efficiency concerns in their defence of centralisation, are in reality expressing value-judgements and adhering to a naïve view of government.

Under free trade, national and local taxes become merely fees for national and local public services.[14] In a world where resource movement is unimpeded by trade barriers, taxes and regulations which do not meet this requirement become so costly that they tend to be abandoned. A similar conclusion has been forcefully argued by one analyst[15] in his penetrating interpretation of the famous 1978 Proposition 13 in California. By mandating the strict equalisation of educational spending among California districts, a California court made it impossible for higher local taxes to buy better schools. The decree converted the local property tax from a benefit tax into a costly distortionary tax on capital.[16] Voters in high-demand school districts chose to reduce drastically their reliance on the property tax in consequence of this trend. By a similar process, the decline of the property tax as a source of local school financing in some Canadian provinces coincided with the rise of the spending equal-isation movement. The lasting reliance of local governments on

---

13 Gary S. Becker, 'An Open Door for Immigrants—the Auction', *Wall Street Journal*, 14 October 1992, p.A 14.

14 In the technical jargon of economists, taxes carry no dead-weight losses.

15 W. A. Fischel, 'Did *Serrano* Cause Proposition 13?', *National Tax Journal*, Vol. 42, December 1989, pp. 465-75.

16 To work as fees for services, taxes have to be complemented by a variety of regulations such as zoning in the case of land use: W. A. Fischel, 'Property Taxation and the Tiebout Model: Evidence for the Benefit View from Zoning and Voting', *Journal of Economic Literature*, Vol. 30, March 1992, pp. 171-77.

the property tax is proof that it does not have too many shortcomings.

Optimal Taxation in a Federalist Perspective

The above view of the sensitivity of resource owners to variations in taxes and regulations contrasts with conventional economic reasoning on local property taxation and indeed taxation in general. The conventional opinion is that the more general a tax is, the more efficient it will be. Local and specific taxes on a single factor like real property are viewed as distortionary.

However, the supposed virtue of general and centralised taxes is that it is harder for taxpayers to avoid the displeasure of paying them by shifting their resources from high-tax jurisdictions to low-tax ones.[17] By contrast, specific taxes and those levied by non-central governments cause economic distortions in inducing victims to attempt evasion by shifting their taxed resources out of the reach of the tax collector.

Conventionally, the capacity of the tax authority to raise revenue is viewed as the criterion of welfare. But that implies a profoundly troubling conception of the state. It is assumed that the tax needs of the government are exogenously determined by the financing requirements of a given optimal quantity of public goods. The orthodox analyst naïvely argues that overall tax rates can be reduced once the base is widened. The analyst is left merely to define the tax arrangement that would efficiently generate such fixed and necessary revenue. Never in this naïve approach is it suggested that the nature of the tax instrument might influence the amount of revenue that the government is willing and able to raise.

Once this equivalent revenue assumption is rejected, a neutral tax (one which minimally influences the behaviour of taxpayers) loses its alleged efficiency. Indeed, the opposite is closer to the truth. In an environment where the largest part of government activity consists in making politically inspired transfers between individuals and groups, taxpayers should more reasonably assume that tax requirements are unlimited. It is difficult to conceive of theoretical or historical limits to the range of favours and privileges that political parties bent on buying votes can devise. To give government access to such vast sources of funds as are implicit in a neutral tax structure is to make the paying

17 Or from taxed resources to untaxed ones within the same jurisdiction.

public vulnerable to the worst excesses of tax authorities. In the extreme case, such tax arrangements render all potential economic value open to confiscation.

Constraining the Tax Leviathan

If this reasoning has any validity, taxpayers should assume that the tax appetite of the Leviathan is better contained when limits are set to their tax exposure. They should reject the assumption of a benevolent despot in search of a fixed and efficient tax budget, and they should be suspicious of further strengthening the government's power to tax. They should incline towards institutional mechanisms which constrain the taxing powers of authorities. One such mechanism consists in narrowing the tax base, via the maximum transfer of taxing powers to decentralised governments. Such a desirable outcome is the consequence of introducing free trade in the community of nations. Once residents of freely trading countries are able to move their resources across national borders, no tax can be raised on a resource which is not compensated by an equivalent benefit to its owners. Rather than being confined to shifting their resources from lawful to unlawful outlets within given territories, individuals can now lawfully shift them between countries.

Whereas some analysts view the widening of the tax base as a desirable attribute of the tax structure, in a more realistic model of the political process, the virtue of a comprehensive base evaporates. We are thus witness to a vast dialogue of the deaf. On the one hand, we hear politicians, bureaucrats, and their spokesmen rage against loopholes and argue in favour of relaxing constraints on the taxing powers of the government, in favour of widening the tax base and in favour of concentrating the power to tax in the hands of centralised governments. On the other hand, ordinary citizens-taxpayers are seen resisting attempts to enlarge the latitude of the tax authorities. As they hold a view of the government closer to the one expressed above, they seek ways to check its tax appetite and shield some valued goods and activities from the reach of the tax collector.

Contrary to the teachings of simplistic economic doctrine, it is desirable to confine the government to so-called 'inefficient' sources of revenue, in allowing taxpayers to remove their wealth from the reach of authorities which do not offer compensating benefits in return. This desirable outcome ensues from the advent of free trade, since national governments then have to compete with one another to attract and hold productive resources within their borders.

Once resources are free to move across national boundaries, the pressure intensifies on national governments to pursue policies that attract rather than repel people and firms. Decentralisation forces governments to match services with variations in demand and in cost. The list of effects that differentiate situations with free trade from conditions without, could be lengthened at will. But the message remains the same: inefficient decisions cost more in a more open economy, because goods, capital and people can more freely move away from the country which imposes unfavourable legislation. National governments have been able to exercise their cartelising influence over the economy mainly because they have had the power to impede the free movement of resources between their boundaries and the rest of the world. And as government decisions are eventually reflected in increased taxes or regulations, the overall impact of free trade on national governments is toward reduced and more neutral taxes and regulations than would otherwise be the case.[18] This process is the defining characteristic of federalism.

[18] As a further illustration of this process as applied to Canadian conditions, see J.-L. Migué, 'True Independence Through Free Trade', in M. Gold and P. Leyton-Brown (eds.), *Trade-offs on Free Trade*, Toronto: Carswell, 1988, pp. 446-53, and Migué, 'Canadian Activists in Solidarity Against Trade Bill', *Wall Street Journal*, 24 April 1987, p. 11.

III. FREE TRADE AS THE DETERMINING
FEATURE OF FEDERALISM

Formal and Effective Federalist Structures

Analysis of competitive governments leads to a questioning of conventional legalistic concepts of federalism as applied to traditional national federations and formal unions of the European type. Observed constitutional federations are sub-categories of a more general process. As Section II shows, a federalist process is set in motion whenever free trade prevents any authority from inefficiently regulating or taxing an economy.

The title 'federalism' can be applied to any political structure in which the power of political authorities extends to less than the size of the economy in which resource movement is free of trade barriers. Its competitive action works within national economies in decentralised federal states or among countries associated in common-market arrangements with only limited central powers.

Whether the central layer of government is made up of elected officials (as in federal states and to some extent in the European Community) or of multinational bodies (as in the Canada-US free-trade area) is analytically immaterial. The determining characteristic of a federalist structure is that most responsibilities are entrusted to decentralised authorities, which have no power to tax or regulate the whole area where trade is free. Such arrangements enhance the ability of resource owners to move their goods, their capital or themselves away from detrimental tax and regulatory measures. Freer trade places national governments approximately in the position of a province, a state or a canton *vis-à-vis* the national economy in a federal state.

The provision of remaining public goods, which can be offered only by the collective action of member-states, is carried out through a body of institutions, whose decisions are binding on national authorities and private agents in the whole bloc. International treaties and agreements can indeed be viewed as arrangements for the provision of public goods common to more than one country. Norad, Nato, the OECD, the agreement on acid rain between the United States and Canada, the IMF, even the United Nations or the binational commissions to settle disputes between New Zealand and Australia or between Canada and the United States are as much central entities as the federal government of Switzerland or the European Commission and associated bodies in Brussels. Multi-track arrangements between governments of a free-trade area allow for co-operation in flexible groupings, while safeguarding the competitive advantage of national autonomy. Multinational bodies have the advantage of being less open to the centralist tendencies of formally federal structures.[1] Indeed, they offer a possible route to federalisation of the world.

Public Goods, State Monopolies and the Federalist Solution

There are two mechanisms for expressing individual preferences—private markets and political action. The first is based on mobility. People reveal their preferences by their decisions to enter or leave an industry or an occupation. The intensity of my preference for clothing, for example, will be reflected in my decision to buy more (enter) or less (exit) of this product.[2] Buyers and sellers are mobile in the sense of having the power to engage in an activity or to avoid it. The concepts of consumer sovereignty and market efficiency always include this condition of freedom of movement by individuals, consumers and producers.

Politics relies on voice to reveal individual preferences. The vote I give in favour of or against such and such a cause, the protest march in which I participate, the lobbying in which I engage, are activities which rely on voice. The exit option does not exist. Citizens may abstain from participating or they may

---

[1] This is not to say that institutional arrangements between member-states do not matter in other respects. For instance, some authors have argued that loose structures may be less stable than tightly controlled federations. Historical experience and analysis indicate that in the trade-off between the alleged instability of loosely-joined federations and the inefficiency of strong central authorities, competition is the choice to be preferred in present world conditions. For a review of this strand of analysis, see W. H. Riker, *The Development of American Federalism*, Boston: Kluwer Academic Publishers, 1987.

[2] The approach is the one taken by A. O. Hirschman in *Exit, Voice and Loyalty*, Cambridge, Mass.: Harvard University Press, 1970.

engage in unlawful activities, but they cannot easily leave the boundaries of the civil society to escape the consequences of political decisions which do not suit them. They are assumed to be immobile.

This assumption of immobility, combined with the character-istics of pure public goods and joint supply, suggests that only a collective decision (voice), and not the entry and exit process, can express preferences for public goods. In economics, a pure public good is defined by the prohibitively high cost of excluding any person from consuming or enjoying it, once it is offered to someone (for example, national defence). Joint supply occurs when one or more factors are highly indivisible; it follows that the marginal cost is lower than the average cost (for instance, the service of a bridge over a river), with the result that the production unit must attain a minimum size (up to a monopoly) to become efficient. In conventional teachings, provision of such goods by the state is the sole mechanism capable of minimising transaction costs, since the co-operation of large numbers of people is necessary for the production or co-ordination of such an indivisible good. Because the decision to clean up a river, to enforce private contracts or to rename a street after a deceased politician, affects large segments of the population and no one may escape the impact of these decisions, only a collective process is assumed capable of reflecting the will of the people. Efficiency is then said to impose a collective process of preference revelation. In democratic societies, this process corresponds to majority voting and political activities in general.

Collectivism in Public Goods: The Prisoner's Dilemma

Nevertheless, public goods provision by the state has been increasingly criticised. This argument for the legitimacy of the state rests on the assumption that all individuals want these collective goods and yet it is not rational for individuals voluntarily to contribute to secure a collectively rational outcome. The public goods problem is often formulated in terms of the *'prisoner's dilemma'** — a game in which each player (individuals in a community) can either co-operate or defect and receive a pay-off based on the other's choice. While the public goods tradition argues that the safest strategy is mutual defection, it has been shown that repeated plays can lead to voluntary collaboration.[3]

---

[3] Robert Axelrod, *The Evolution of Cooperation*, New York: Basic Books, 1984, and Michael Taylor, *The Possibility of Cooperation*, Cambridge: Cambridge University Press, 1987.

Provision by the state also implies forcing some to pay for other people's services, which is hard to justify on ethical grounds.

A recent book on this question[4] concludes that this version of the public goods argument at best rests on paternalism. In the author's words, if we know there are no 'honest hold-outs', unanimity in a voluntary contract becomes possible. If, on the other hand, there are honest hold-outs but we cannot identify them, then we may need coercion; but coercive production by the state implies forcing some people to pay for other people's projects. Another line of analysis[5] questioning the assumed superiority of coercive provision of public goods argues that the strategy with the largest pay-off in a game involving repeated plays is the tit-for-tat strategy.

> 'The two key requisites for co-operation to thrive are that the co-operation be based on reciprocity, and that the shadow of the future is important enough to make this reciprocity stable',

the author writes (p. 173). In the conventional language of economists, it appears rational for individuals to contribute voluntarily to secure a public good and to revert to tit-for-tat when history indicates that other individuals would not repeatedly co-operate. Under free trade, coercion is unnecessary in the provision of some public goods. In other words, the 'prisoner's dilemma' can be avoided in a large number of cases traditionally assumed to call for public provision.

In practical terms, the political process is costly and imperfect as a means of revealing demand. *Rent-seeking** activities lead to governments expanding into redistributive activities well beyond those allowed them by their public goods mandate; thus the public provision of services (such as health care and education) poses the problem of state monopoly and coercion. More than market monopoly, state monopoly is to be avoided. Some efficiency loss from multiple supply becomes socially acceptable if it is offset by gains from lessened coercion.

Centralisation, 'Harmonisation' and Small Nations

One empirical observation is particularly significant. The absence of any relationship between *per capita* income and the size of national economies has led some economists to suggest

---

[4] David Schmidtz, *The Limits of Government : An Essay on the Public Goods Argument*, Boulder, Colorado: Westview Press, 1991.

[5] Axelrod, *op. cit.*

that the public goods argument for centralisation and harmon-isation beyond national levels may not be very compelling.[6] As long as they have access to the benefits of international trade, it seems that small nations can perform as well economically as big ones. Little relationship is observed between the optimum market size and the optimum size of the political unit. The advantage of being in a position to spread the cost of public goods (such as defining a legal system) over a larger base of taxpayers may not be decisive.

Moreover, there is another consideration, relevant to examin-ation of the federalist process, which should be emphasised. The boundaries of public goods are not necessarily fixed, and demanders of public goods may not be immobile. Pure public goods are often limited in space. They may be 'public' only at the regional or national level, without having pronounced *spillover effects** on neighbouring communities. Even where spillovers are observed, some efficiency loss from decentralis-ation can be offset by gains from lessened coercion. In these numerous cases of quasi-public goods—such as education, roads, environmental amenities—exit (mobility) is an alternative to voice (politics). The movement of goods, capital and people between communities reintroduces competition into the public sector. A form of market for public goods may then emerge as a substitute for the political process. Under free trade and for a large number of public services, an alternative to govern-ment coercion exists and the public goods 'problem' can be circumvented via federalism, which is the counterpart of the market in the public sector because it institutionalises com-petition among governments. While traditionally used to describe competition within national federal states, the model applies equally well to national governments of freely-trading countries.

Voluntary Association of Individuals in Diversified Communities

In federalist structures, the ideal of voluntary exchange may be realised in the public sector through the voluntary association of individuals in what the economic literature has come to designate

---

[6] On this see R. J. Barro, 'Small is Beautiful', *Wall Street Journal*, 11 October 1991, and G. S. Becker, 'Actually, Small-Fry Nations Can Do Just Fine', *Business Week*, 1 October 1990.

clubs[7] and communities.[8] Traditional analysis of federalism (associated with the *'Tiebout approach'**) relies solely on the movement of people as the mechanism to discipline local governments, to the almost total exclusion of goods and capital mobility, but the latter two channels of competition can only strengthen the *Tiebout process**, and at best converge towards the same end-result.

The exclusion of those who do not pay for their portion of the consumption of indivisible goods occurs in a federal structure through the mechanism of distance which serves as the means of exclusion when the consumption of a public service requires presence in a particular area. When a number of these bundles of public goods is offered at numerous national locations within a larger economic community (such as the European Community or the North American Free Trade Area), the population will divide spatially into communities made up of people with similar tastes, who choose to live in a given national community precisely because it offers them a constellation of natural amenities and public services adapted to their preferences. Under the best conditions, the full diversity of public preferences is revealed through immigration of individuals into communities that correspond to their tastes and emigration from communities that do not, using the silent mechanism of 'voting with the feet' well known to economists. Each national community becomes a sort of club and all of the clubs constitute the civil society (the federation).

In principle, a world made up of such national communities is more apt to achieve efficiency, namely the concordance of services with the preferences of the population as a whole. Each person more easily finds the combination of services and tax burden that best corresponds to his or her vision of the good society.[9] Responsibility is imposed on public decision-makers by

---

[7] Originally formulated by James Buchanan in 'An Economic Theory of Clubs', *Economica*, Vol. 32, February 1965, pp. 1-14. The notion of clubs as a mechanism for revealing preferences in public goods is not in itself limited to geographical proximity. As our subject, federalism, revolves around this dimension in particular, it is this variety of clubs that we will focus on. This statement is not strictly valid even though it is generally verifiable in practice. For example, a proposal was advanced to constitute the numerous separated Aboriginal communities of Canada into a single province.

[8] A tradition introduced by C. M. Tiebout, 'A Pure Theory of Local Expenditures', *Journal of Political Economy*, Vol. 64, October 1956, pp. 416-24.

[9] In economist's language, in every country the tax price converges toward the willingness of taxpayers to pay for the public goods offered.

the ability of people to shield themselves from policies that do not suit them. Federalism relies on mobility to realise efficiency, reserving for each region or nation the responsibility for decisions that concern solely its citizens. In a federalist structure, each region assumes the cost of its policies.

Federalism Without Full Population Mobility

The 'Tiebout process' is not perfect, just as market competition and political competition are never perfect. A good deal of the criticism levelled at the competitive federalist model is simply based on the assertion that it is not perfect. But that says nothing useful, since every human action testifies to a lack of perfect knowledge and mobility. To evaluate a federalist order by the theoretical model of perfect government competition between national communities is no more valid than to assess private markets by the theoretical model of perfect competition. It is necessary to explain how real-world commercial and political markets work.

In addition to this superficial criticism of the Tiebout tradition, the economic literature alludes to two other weaknesses. Among several conditions assumed necessary to ensure optimal provision of local or national public goods under federalism, full mobility of the population and the absence of scale economies in producing the public goods are two of the more important ones. However, while population mobility enhances the federalist adjustment process, it is in general not essential for the construction of an international federalist order. Mobility of goods and capital is often sufficient. The mobility of people is not the only force in the competitive process among governments.

The Tiebout model has been interpreted formally as requiring that the population be divided into different local or national clubs, each of which has homogeneous tastes or incomes. Within each jurisdiction, all individuals pay the same amount of taxes for the same amount of public services. Such a result obviously implies full mobility of citizens and perfect knowledge of the characteristics of all communities. But this condition is unduly restrictive for a reasonable working of the competitive process between jurisdictions.

To facilitate the expression of people's preferences for public goods in real-world conditions, homogeneity is unnecessary even in theory.[10] With some mobility of persons at the margin, taxes on various groups within national communities tend to evolve towards neutrality or as a function of benefits received from the consumption of public goods. No matter the income group to which individuals belong, at the margin they will tend to be attracted to communities offering benefits higher than taxes and will move away from those offering the opposite combination. The whole system tends to converge towards a structure where individuals receive marginal benefits equal to their tax per unit of public goods.[11]

Moreover, once barriers to trade are removed, it is not necessary to assume some mobility of people and firms between jurisdictions because of the tendency for factor prices to equalise under free trade.

How does this factor price equalisation theorem (outlined in Box 1) relate to the alleged problem of people immobility among national communities and the inability of national governments to deviate from benefit taxes on people and factors? The link is as follows. National governments of freely trading countries cannot influence national gross factor incomes, even when factors such as land and labour are immobile. Factor prices are entirely determined outside national economies via the mobility of commodities. This implies that, without trade barriers, population mobility is often not necessary to persuade national governments to adopt regulations and taxes that are compensated by equivalent benefits. Should governments act otherwise, they set in motion a whole series of consequences which could not be long sustained.

Land Is Not Immobile

Suppose, for instance, a national government elects to raise taxes on an immobile factor such as land. It is claimed by some that

[10] In the particular case of local property taxes, it has been shown that marginal taxes paid tend towards equality with marginal willingness to pay for local services, even in heterogeneous communities. (B. W. Hamilton, 'Capitalisation of Intrajurisdictional Differences in Local Tax Prices', *American Economic Review*, Vol. 66, December 1976, pp. 743-53; also W. A. Fischel, 'Property Taxation and the Tiebout Model', *op. cit.*)

[11] In the best of circumstances the Samuelson condition for efficiency in the provision of public goods would be satisfied in heterogeneous communities. Purists argue that individual members of all clubs could increase their welfare even more by moving to communities with equal taxes. Analysts of real-world markets will respond that the best is often the enemy of the good. Empirical evidence suggests that reduced dispersion of incomes within the local polity tends to set in. On this point, see G. Miller, *Cities by Contract*, Cambridge, Mass.: MIT Press, 1981, mostly in chs. 6 and 7.

[34]

Equalising Factor Prices

The 'factor price equalisation theorem'[1] states that, provided commodities can move freely between countries, real factor prices move towards the same level in all countries, *even when factors of production cannot move*. The theorem rests on the proposition that a unique configuration of factor earnings corresponds to each commodity price ratio. Suppose, for instance, that the demand for high-technology goods expands on world markets. As the production of such commodities expands in a given country, upward pressure is put on the hiring and the price of factors such as electronic engineers that are intensively used in that industry.[2] The same competitive forces cause the skilled-unskilled labour proportions to adjust in other industries as well. This change in the skilled-unskilled proportions of labour in turn leads to an increase in the relative incomes of skilled labour in all industries in all trading nations. In the final analysis, a unique set of factor proportions and a unique set of skilled-unskilled wages can be inferred for all countries. Changes in commodity price ratios in world markets cause corresponding movements in factor earnings in national economies, which in turn result in changes in the proportion of various factors employed in domestic and foreign industries.

[1] Paul A. Samuelson, 'International Trade and the Equalization of Factor Prices', *Economic Journal*, Vol. 58, June 1948, pp. 163-84.

[2] Recent changes in the demand for human-capital-intensive goods did cause a substantial decline in the incomes of low-skill labour relative to high-skill workers in most industrial nations.

the remuneration of such an immobile factor is a rent and therefore bears the entire burden of the tax. Immobile factor owners supposedly cannot be protected from abuse by the government. It has, however, been shown[12] that factor owners are far from powerless. The notion of mobility, as commonly used, connotes the ability to move physically and/or geographically. But when properly used in economic analysis, it refers instead to the ability of a factor to be substituted from one

[12] Most forcefully by J. Vernon Henderson, 'The Tiebout Model: Bring Back the Entrepreneurs', *Journal of Political Economy*, Vol. 93, April 1985, pp. 248-64.

use to another even though it may be physically immovable. Used in this sense, standard taxation analysis holds that if land is discriminately taxed on the basis of the use to which it is put (housing or vacant), then its remuneration is no longer a rent. Entrepreneurs will see that it is shifted from one use to another on the basis of its tax burden. In those conditions, land is not an immobile factor.

Land can also be used in one community rather than another. As argued by Henderson, if land in one territory earns less than in a neighbouring community (because of differential taxation or otherwise), land owners will use it less intensively in the first community and more intensively in the neighbouring one. Net land prices will be equalised across communities just as they are equalised across competing uses. Two recent illustrations come to mind. Some years ago, New York City had to back down on its proposal to raise the property tax on Madison Square Garden, as the sports facility owners threatened to move their activity to neighbouring New Jersey. In similar fashion, following a decision by Ontario Hydro to resort to peak-load pricing of its electricity in winter, some industrial users elected to move their operations to neighbouring Quebec during the high-price season. To alleviate pressure on its own facilities, Quebec Hydro also had to revert to differential winter pricing.

It is therefore clear that, when goods or services are free to move across territories, owners of 'immobile' factors are protected from extortionary taxes or regulations. While the process is not as powerful at the international level, the number of communities and their size can be influenced by relative tax burdens or service quality. Whether this mechanism is enough fully to protect resource owners is an empirical question not resolved in this paper. Varying intensity in the use of immobile labour may not be as feasible as when land is the immobile factor. On the other hand, the movement of labour within emerging blocs is clearly not negligible. That the movement of goods implies some protection for owners of 'immobile' factors is sufficient to validate the position taken here. In the real world of trading blocs, capital and labour are of course also mobile.

Conclusion: Free Trade Prevents Extortionate Taxes and Excessive Regulation

The conclusion is as follows. Should a national government raise taxes or regulations on a physically immobile factor such as

[36]

land, this will in the short term cause a reduction in the use of land. The movement is equivalent to a downward shift in the supply of land in the home country. A related rise will then occur in the price of land-intensive commodities within national boundaries. But if there is free trade with the outside world, such a rise is impossible. Foreign suppliers will flood the domestic market of the land-intensive commodity, wiping out the national industry. Only taxes and regulations compensated by equivalent benefits are generally consistent with free trade in goods and services.

The assumption of full population mobility is therefore unduly restrictive for the reasonable operation of the competitive process between national governments within common markets. Competitive federalism is not uniquely dependent on population mobility. Residents of national economies can be protected from abuse by national governments through the sole action of goods movement with the outside world. But competition follows several channels. The effective mobility of capital and people in emerging blocs enhances the power of this process and constrains the ability of governments to affect domestic factor prices or earnings.

Inefficient Migrations as Rent-Seeking

Just as too little mobility of people is alleged to hamper the working of the process of competitive federalism, others claim that competive federalism is vitiated by *too much* mobility. This view relates to assumed scale economies in the production of national public goods as well as differential rental incomes between national or local communities. As the cost of the public good is spread over a larger number of persons, each entrant into a national or local community contributes to lowering the cost of producing the pure public good. From the individual's standpoint, the marginal benefits of moving to the larger community exceed those of staying, because the external costs imposed on those left behind are not taken into account. Thus population movements are set in motion, not because they improve the geographical distribution of the population, but because they allow movers to share in the rent of residing in larger communities.

Similar consequences are said to follow from the presence of higher rental income in some locations. The benefits of increased tax revenue to finance the provision of public goods are greater in national communities with higher resource rents to tap. When the distribution of locational rents differs among communities, inefficient migration towards regions or countries most endowed in environmental or other rental resources is allegedly encouraged.

Allegedly inefficient migrations between communities are really a specific application of the more general consequences on entry of the incomplete assignment of *property rights**[13] in resources. To illustrate, let us assume that a country or a region is endowed with a rich variety of water streams favourable to the generation of electric power. Revenues raised by market prices to owners of generating facilities are received as private property by well-specified owners.[14] One can become a resource user only by first purchasing the right from current owners. Claimants to the revenue from market prices do not compete over how the product of the resource rent is distributed after it is raised. Rent-seeking is ruled out, because there is no expected return from this *negative-sum game**. Competition among resource owners leads to the efficient allocation of the resource in response to consumer preferences and production costs and as such is wealth maximising.

The outcome differs in the presence of rent-seeking over the distribution of the revenues raised by taxes levied on privately-owned facilities. Raising taxes on the rent of a physical facility is effectively the same as nationalising an equivalent portion of the resource. Government programmes financed by such levies generate benefits whose distribution is determined by political competition among rival interest groups after taxes have been raised. Scarce resources are devoted to a competition for the existing wealth. One form this competition takes is excess entry by individuals and firms into the territory under the jurisdiction of the taxing government. In general, revenues raised by government taxes typically go into a fund made available to the public in expanded services. The beneficiaries of these revenues are left unspecified.[15] Simply by moving into the territory (which

---

[13] For an examination of its implications for environmental resources and policies, see Jean-Luc Migué and Richard Marceau, 'Pollution Taxes, Subsidies and Rent Seeking', *Canadian Journal of Economics*, Vol. 25, May 1993.

[14] Ownership rights are said to be specified in the sense that they are assigned to a closed class of entities: see C. G. Holderness, 'The Assignment of Rights, Entry Effects, and the Allocation of Resources', *Journal of Legal Studies*, Vol. 18, January 1989, pp. 181-90.

[15] Titles on this portion of the taxed resource are said to be assigned to an open class.

will involve some costs), individuals and firms can benefit from tax revenues without first purchasing rights from current residents of the territory.

Relative to a situation with complete assignment of property rights to well-specified owners, all policy options[16] give rise to rent-seeking. In terms of control over the revenue raised on a resource rent, a basic distinction must therefore be made between market prices for resources on the one hand and government taxes on these resources on the other. Programmes like subsidies to regional development are offered in such a manner that potential beneficiaries are often rewarded to enter or stay in a region. Competition for the appropriation of these transfers takes the form of excess entry and output in those regions.

Efficiency Implications

The efficiency implications of this process for the federalist arrangement can now be derived. A national or local tax on rental incomes can result in migrations towards regions most endowed in environmental or other rental resources within the common market. Because resources are in different locations, appropriation by national governments of higher rental income can result in the familiar migration problem, when the distribution of rents differs between members of a common market.[17]

The standard method proposed to achieve the socially optimal distribution of population consists of entrusting a central authority with the task of preventing inefficient migrations by levying taxes and offering subsidies on the movement in and out of communities. Two factors militate against this approach. First, it is naïve to assume that competition over the product of centrally-levied taxes will be less serious than competition via migration for regionally levied taxes. Theoretically, the opposite result is more likely in view of the increased monopoly power held by central taxing authorities. After all, migration is just one

---

16 This is nothing more than a simple extension of A. Krueger's seminal paper on the implications of rent-seeking for policy choices. (A. Krueger, 'The Political Economy of the Rent-Seeking Society', *American Economic Review*, Vol. 64, June 1974, pp. 291-303.)

17 Ever since the advent of the so-called oil crisis in the 1970s, which meant immense wealth to the oil-rich province of Alberta, such ideas have served as the backbone of the centralist position in Canada. It has also inspired policy prescriptions in favour of centrally-imposed taxes rather than subsidies to polluters in the allocation of environmental resources.

avenue whereby rent-seeking can take place. Faith in the ability of central governments to allocate populations on the basis of efficiency requirements rests on a public-interest view of central governments. As tax avoidance is made more difficult once the power to tax is centralised, central planning of population movements is likely to result in higher tax and spending budgets and more rent-seeking. Even assuming that the central authority has the information necessary to choose the right tax and subsidy levels, there is no guarantee that it will do so. When transfers across communities are institutionalised, pressure group politics also becomes institutionalised. As the theory of rent-seeking holds, no public intervention, let alone intervention by a central authority, can be free from competition over the distribution of rents.

In practice, a less ominous alternative, more consistent with the spirit of federalism, and more likely to overcome rent-seeking by migration, is available. It consists in vesting local communities and national governments in common markets with full property rights to natural characteristics and differential rental incomes. Their power to tax and regulate migrations in and out of their territory on the basis of local benefits available, would provide the same efficiency outcome as the idealised central solution, without its dangers. Individuals under this régime would be forced to internalise the cost of their decision to move or to stay. No example can better illustrate the working of this process than the ability of municipal governments to align tax contributions on benefits received by taxpayers though, as argued earlier,[18] this process is not exclusive to local governments.

---

[18] Above, pp. 21-26.

IV. CENTRALISATION VERSUS FEDERALISM

Decentralisation *vs.* Centralisation

The competitive model examined above comes into play without legal or constitutional limits on the legislative power of national governments, provided the mobility of resources is not hampered. In a decentralised system, exit not voice is the ultimate instrument by which individuals make their preferences known. But the power of exit works only if national decisions are not over-ridden by a central power covering the same fields, within trade blocs or at the supra-national level.

Centralisation is defined as the power of a central authority to rule over an entire common-market economy employing taxes, spending programmes and regulation. Thus it neutralises the competitive process of federalism. What use is the freedom to leave a province or a country, what use is the choice that consumers have to purchase their goods from outside suppliers, if the central government can regulate and tax the economy at the common-market level? Individuals and groups bound by country A no longer have the option to escape its restrictions by emigrating to country B, or by moving their capital and assets elsewhere, since the federalist solution is thwarted by the central cartel. Resource mobility cannot act as a mechanism to shield resources from unfavourable legislation and as an avenue for productive adjustment. It is no accident that throughout history despotic régimes have deemed it necessary to control tightly the movement of resources across their borders.

Centralisation weakens the power citizens have over their government and opens the way for interest groups and rent seekers to obtain transfers at the expense of the rest of the population. As local or national economies are more open than the common-market economy, central government possesses monopolistic powers which decentralised administrations cannot emulate. Only it has the power to change relative prices within the common market. It is this difference in monopoly power that inspires most economists to favour decentralisation: the powers lost by central government as devolution increases are recovered only partially (or not at all) by the decentralised authorities. The citizens come out the winners.

The Meaning of 'Federalism'

Paradoxically, in the conventional debate in federal states and in Europe, 'federalism' is associated with the strengthening of the central government's powers, while the search for autonomy and decentralisation is linked to narrow secessionist movements and anti-European options. Supporters of devolution are immediately labelled anti-Europe and 'nation-builders'. Yet the contrary is true. Federalism is decentralisation. As a form of government, federalism is the opposite, not of decentralisation, but of the unitary state. The partisans of devolution are the real federalists.

A conventional assessment of the Savings and Loans crisis in the United States[1] illustrates the confusion. In a perfectly perverse use of language, the author designates by the label 'fiscal federalism' the arrangement whereby depositors in Texas received $20 billion in deposit insurance, whilst the US Treasury collected only $1·3 billion in taxes from Savings and Loans Institutions in that state. There are two assumptions implicit in this judgement. First, federalism is measured not by the extent of decentralisation and competition but by its opposite, the power of a central authority to neutralise these two forces. Second, it is wrongly assumed that the government of a unitary state could not have done even better in terms of redistribution in favour of some regional interests.

Unfortunately, such centralist visions have become mainstream teaching among economists. In their assessment of the proposed unified European currency, two recognised authorities argue that such a plan could result in very serious strains, unless some type of EC-wide tax-transfer scheme is put in place.[2] Their idealised model is the United States of America where the federal government absorbs, in reduced taxes and increased transfers, up to 40 per cent of any decline in a typical region's income. In contrast the European Community, they lament, merely cushions 0·5 per cent of the impact of an adverse shock.

It has also been argued that special-interest groups in Europe

---

[1] Barry Eichengreen, *Is Europe an Optimum Currency Area?*, NBER Working Paper No. 3579, January 1991, pp. 24-25.

[2] Jeffrey Sachs and Xavier Sala-i-Martin, *Fiscal Federalism and Optimum Currency Area: Evidence for Europe from the United States*, NBER Working Paper No. 3855, October 1991.

today may have more influence on national governments than on the central authority in Brussels.[3] If so, partisans of the free market should support conferring more power, not less, on Eurocrats. But this is a short-term perspective, possibly valid during the transitional phase towards a full-fledged constitutional central authority. On the other hand, both the history of federal structures and economic analysis[4] show that it takes time for rent-seeking to become institutionalised. Furthermore, after the common market is in place, rent-seeking activities at the national level can be expected to die out because of declining returns on investments in political action at that level. National governments under free trade lose their power to redistribute wealth arbitrarily. Europeans have a unique opportunity at this time to heed those lessons, in taking care to avoid establishing central redistributionist machinery.

'Balkanising' Common Markets by Centralisation

An idea widely held by politicians, bureaucrats and some economists is that only a strong central authority can safeguard the economic union of a common market against narrow protectionist interests. However, history and analysis show that the central governments of existing federations or a strong central authority in Europe can and do use their monopoly power over the common market to 'balkanise' the economy by erecting insuperable international barriers between member-states. A strong central authority is far more able to balkanise a common market than individual member-states.[5]

The process is as follows. By virtue of their inability to affect outside prices, member-states by themselves cannot shift the cost of inefficient decisions to other members of the common market. Given the mobility of resources, they have no choice but to assume the burden of costly policies. Thus national governments (or provinces) constantly face constraints on their ability to distort prices and balkanise the economy. The federal govern-

---

3 See D. Brooks, 'Europe Muddles toward a Freer Market', *Wall Street Journal*, 14 December 1990.

4 We are referring in particular to Mancur Olson's thesis that when a new common interest group emerges, resources for the lobbying organisation may not be forthcoming immediately. (See M. Olson, *The Rise and Decline of Nations: Economic Growth, Stagflation and Rigidities*, New Haven, Con.: Yale University Press, 1984.)

5 For an application of this line of analysis to the Canadian federation, see Jean-Luc Migué, 'The Balkanization of the Canadian Economy, A Legacy of Federal Policies', in Filip Palda (ed.), [title not yet decided], Vancouver, BC: The Fraser Institute (forthcoming).

ment of a union operates under leaner constraints, inasmuch as it possesses the power to rule over the entire economic union behind trade barriers.

The degree of balkanisation can be measured by the extent to which government intervention dissociates the price or tax burden of regional goods and services from their production cost. Inasmuch as prices are determined at common-market level, such distortions can be caused only by central intervention acting over the whole community behind trade barriers. Only a central authority can shift the burden of a policy to non-national victims. The distortion is no less real when prices of publicly-supplied goods and services, such as education or health services, rather than market prices, are distorted. Balkanising a common market is equivalent to erecting tariffs, quotas and protectionist subsidies between the member-states of a common market.

Inter-Regional Price Distortions Through Central Supply

In a centralised régime, supply by a supra-national authority is substituted for national supply, either directly or indirectly as when equalisation hand-outs are offered and costs are shared with member-states. The allocation method favoured by central governments is service uniformity over the whole territory at a quality level approximating the preferences of the median voter for the community as a whole. Under a system that does away with regional responsibility, the output distribution is made more uniform across regions. Instead of reflecting regional demand and cost conditions, as in a true federal system, the tax price is increased (through uniform proportional and progressive taxation) in upper-income regions and lowered in low-income areas. In effect, the central authority practices price discrimination but among regions rather than among different consumers of a given industry.

The centralised provision of public services provides implicit subsidies to less-developed members of the common market. Selling public services on the cheap to lower-income countries is no different from offering subsidies to producers or exporters in those countries. In reducing regional production costs, the practice hinders the process of resource specialisation and acts as a protectionist measure in favour of lagging areas. By contrast, production costs are raised in the most productive countries as a result of the increased tax burden.

[44]

Standardisation by central supply is a form of tie-in sale whereby people in high-demand regions are coerced into sharing the desired output with people in low-demand areas: the central authority collects part of the consumer's surplus from high-demand buyers to transfer it to median-income consumers. Only the central authority possesses the monopoly power necessary to operate such transfers. Although excess centralisation has generally been ascribed to bureaucratic pressures and producers' interests, factor suppliers can receive enthusiastic support for centralisation from consumers in nations most likely to gain from the standardisation of output across the territory.[6] As explained above (p. 18), the Irish referendum campaign on Maastricht was almost entirely fought on that ground.[7]

Inter-Regional Price Distortions Through Central Hand-outs

Two further instruments are available to the central government of a common market to pursue discriminatory pricing goals: payments to decentralised governments and central regulation. Assume that the central authority of a federal state or a common market subsidises the local consumption of a service (say, education or road services) through equalisation grants or cost-sharing agreements. Such arrangements lower the prices of education or road services below cost in lagging regions and raise them above cost elsewhere. The marginal benefit of education is lower than its cost for the former, higher in the latter areas. Central hand-outs distort preferences; they carry inter-regional transfers with them and hamper the specialisation of resources. When offered by the central authority of a common market, they act as national trade barriers in favour of lagging countries.

In a true federalist structure, such violation of true price-cost ratios across areas of a common market would bring the mobility process into action. National member-states of the common market which raised taxes above the value of services (as perceived by their residents) would soon find that resources

---

[6] For a more systematic analysis of centralist pressures originating from consumers in a specific federal structure, see L. S. Wilson, 'The Socialization of Medical Insurances in Canada', *Canadian Journal of Economics*, Vol. 18, May 1985, pp. 355-76. This view is in turn grounded in the more general theory of government size as developed in A. H. Meltzer and S. F. Richard, 'A Rational Theory of the Size of Government', *Journal of Political Economy*, Vol. 89, October 1981, pp. 914-27.

[7] The Irish were literally bought (to the tune of an estimated $12 billion-worth of aid and special benefits), because the Continent could not be allowed to plunge into turmoil.

were repelled from their territory; but that is not so under a centralist arrangement. By virtue of the uniform tax régime implemented at common-market level, productive resources in prosperous areas have no incentives to move away from jurisdictions burdened by their excess share of the common education or road programmes. Furthermore, producers in subsidised territories are encouraged to stay in their less productive employment by the education cartel at common-market level. Central hand-outs are protectionist, causing national or regional prices to be dissociated from regional costs. Equalising government services at the common-market level is equivalent to cross-subsidising regionally rather than at the industry level, inhibiting the specialisation of the community's resources.

Variable hand-outs to investments and infrastructures in regions result in similar distortions. Granting investment tax credits to designated areas, like direct subsidies to public services, results in expenditures being made for the benefit of certain regional groups and at the expense of others, irrespective of their net profitability. Centralisation is in effect the dissociation of regional prices from regional costs, resulting in the further balkanisation of the common-market economy: it is essentially a trade barrier.

The same can be said of practices such as central government procurement policies. When a supra-regional government purchases a supply of inputs in one region rather than another, even though it is more expensive, then it is balkanising the economy. By paying more than minimum cost, it transfers wealth to some holders of regional factors, while imposing additional burdens (prices) on taxpayers/consumers in other areas. Consequently it inhibits specialisation of the community's resources and restricts trade.

Inter-Regional Price Distortions Through Central Regulation

The irony of the centralist vision of Europe is that, while central provision of public services, cost-sharing and regional-development policies would result in lower resource mobility and excess population in declining areas, social and economic regulation by the central authority would imply reduced investment and population in less prosperous countries. The proposed social charter with its alleged rights to standardised health, education and social-insurance services, with its support

[46]

for uniform environmental standards, with its goal of imposing common union wages and working conditions (affirmative action programmes), would have two important consequences. First, it would cause production costs to rise throughout the Community. Second, the common standards would be set by interest groups in the most developed and prosperous urbanised regions. The ability of lower-income, lagging areas to compete with the most productive ones would therefore be reduced. Poorer regions would be denied the power to compete with prosperous ones through lower wages, lower taxes or fewer environmental amenities.

Consider, for instance, the impact of imposing common working wages, uniform affirmative action policies and collective bargaining rules throughout the common market. By raising labour costs proportionately more in lagging areas, such policies act as specific taxes on labour in less productive countries. In effect, they would be tariffs on the importation of capital into countries that need it most. Similarly, extending common environmental standards to the less-developed countries of the European community would raise the cost of doing business in those locations and reduce capital movements into those places, just like additional tariffs on capital imports. Defying all commonsense but not surprisingly, opposition to the North American Free Trade Area comes in large part from Canadian and American 'environmentalists' and organised labour, who fear the expansion of opportunities in Mexico. In similar fashion, imposing standardised health and welfare services on all employers across the common market would result in higher production costs and taxes in lagging areas. Regulation by the central government of a common market acts as a protectionist instrument for the benefit of interest groups in the more prosperous countries and is clearly a dominant factor in balkanisation.

Yet these initiatives, which impose the uniform treatment of regions in matters of taxation, expenditures and regulations and which are the major forces behind balkanisation, represent a major part of central governments' proposed activity in some emerging common markets, particularly in Europe. The massive expansion of the central power contemplated by some in Europe threatens to distort the functioning of what is envisaged as a federal system. But federalism is not homogenisation. The centralisation which is likely implies balkanisation of the

[47]

common-market economy because all central interventions with pronounced local incidence are equivalent to implicit regional tariffs, regional taxes or discriminatory subsidies to regional consumers and producers.

Cartels of Regional Governments

Redistributive policies of central governments foster resistance to necessary regional adjustments in another way. By releasing member-states from the consequences of their decisions, central subsidies and regulations remove the incentive for provincial or national governments to adopt adjustment policies. Equalisation payments, cost-sharing programmes and central regulatory measures serve to shield decentralised administrations from the consequences of their own cost-increasing policies. All three instruments result in national policy costs being shifted to other parts of the common market. The absurd result would be that the more inefficient national governments are, the more they would be compensated by the central authority.

Should Europe embark on the centralist path, member-states would find themselves free to indulge in distorting practices mostly because the federal authority would stand ready to shift the cost of their policies to outside taxpayers or consumers and to neutralise the federalist adjustment process. Measures such as cost-sharing arrangements, equalisation policies, regional policies and the extension of national regulations to common market scale mostly serve to sterilise the national economic cost implied by national policies. This result is most visible in the case of the proposed European monetary integration where the cost of adjustment by member-states is merely shifted from irresponsible member-states to more conservative and prosperous ones.[8]

Decentralised governments have an incentive to collude. To enforce collusive agreements, the offices of some central, 'higher' authority are required in the form of common trade barriers against the outside world, deductibility of local taxes, revenue and cost sharing and regulation at the common-market level. As evidenced by the Common Agricultural Policy, the lion's share of the Community budget and regulations serves mainly to shelter member-states from the consequences of their own decisions.

[8] This point is discussed at greater length above, pp. 17-20. See also B. L. Benson, 'Interstate Tax Competition, Incentives to Collude, and Federal Influences', *The Cato Journal*, Vol. 10, Spring/Summer 1990, pp. 75-90.

The conclusion to be drawn from past and planned practices of centralised structures is unambiguous. Federal initiatives which impose uniformity in matters of taxation, expenditures and regulations are distortionary and protectionist in nature. All central interventions with variable local incidence are the equivalent of implicit regional customs tariffs, regional quotas or discriminatory subsidies to regional consumers and producers. They all inhibit the specialisation of the community's resources and restrict trade.

Centralising Tendencies of Federal Governments

Centralist forces are always and everywhere at work because centralisation is the natural ally of regional and other interest groups. Only a central authority with power to rule over the entire economy is generally capable of raising implicit trade barriers between regions of the common market by one of three instruments: central supply, central hand-outs or central regulation.[9] This is not a trivial statement, nor should it be taken for granted. Conventional wisdom holds that a strong central government is a prerequisite for the safeguard of the economic union, whereas member-governments are agents of balkanisation. But the opposite is closer to the truth. To entrust the federal government with the task of safeguarding the economic union is to entrust the sheep to the care of the wolf. For fuller European economic integration, political powers in Brussels should be minimised.

Of course, member-states of federations can and often do attempt to raise national or regional trade barriers within the common market principally through procurement practices of national governments and state monopolies, nationalisation of entire sectors such as air or rail transport, state marketing boards (wine in France and Italy), prohibition of land ownership by non-residents and, not least, imposing barriers on the movement of labour (for example, by setting up language and occupational requirements). However, if experience in traditional federations is any guide, the danger originating in decentralised governments is grossly exaggerated. Regional governments in most federal states have been able to indulge in distorting practices mostly because the federal authority has proven adept at

[9] Roland Vaubel, 'The Political Economy of Centralization and the European Community', *Journal des Economistes et des Études Humaines*, Vol. 3, March 1992, pp. 11-48.

neutralising the federalist adjustment process. Analysts of barriers in the Canadian federation conclude that

'it is difficult to predict that central or unitary governments will be less prone to distort internal trade flows than lower levels of government. The evidence ... suggests the opposite'.[10]

'Based on the concept of balkanisation as the distortion of inter-provincial prices by a budget or regulatory intervention, it can be estimated that in 1990, in excess of three-quarters of federal expenditures budgets were regionally distortionary in nature.'[11]

Since over two-thirds of the EC budget is accounted for by the Common Agricultural Policy, the danger of a similar outcome in the young EC federation can hardly be overemphasised.

Referring to the distortions caused by procurement practices of five European national governments,[12] a recent report argues that 'les économies globales, qu'une "ouverture" des marchés publics permettrait de réaliser se situent entre 8 et 19 milliards d'écus'.[13] Protectionism by national governments in Europe is indeed costly and deplorable, but as potential enforcers of implicit collusive agreements between national administrations after 1992, EC budgets and regulations are vastly more dangerous. Certainly the precedent-setting CAP is far from reassuring.

Harmonisation, a Menace to Federalism

One tradition, both in federal states and in the nascent federal structure of Europe, suggests that duplication of functions is pure waste. It is allegedly important to confine regional and national governments clearly to matters well defined by scale economies and spillover effects. At the minimum, arrangements between autonomous jurisdictions should provide for institutionalised policy-harmonisation mechanisms. Such anti-competitive preju-dice, especially when penned by economists, is hard to understand. In a market economy, multiple suppliers are considered desirable and necessary. Multiplicity generally implies

10 M. J. Trebilcock *et al.*, 'Provincially Induced Barriers to Trade in Canada: A Survey', in M. J. Trebilcock *et al.*, *Federalism and the Canadian Economic Union*, Toronto: University of Toronto Press, 1983, p. 558.

11 J.-L. Migué, 'The Balkanization of the Canadian Economy, A Legacy of Federal Policies', *op. cit.*

12 Germany, Belgium, France, Italy and the UK.

13 Paolo Cecchini, *1992, Le Défi*, Commission Européenne, Paris: Flammarion, 1988, p. 70.

a broadening of the range of choices. Why should it be otherwise in the public sector?

Centralisers use this argument to rationalise harmonisation by the central authority, the 'natural' integrator, while autonomy advocates and separatists use it as the basis for their claims in favour of 'devolution'. In the latter case rationalisation of operations through clear-cut assignment of tasks to lower-level authorities is invoked as the goal. In reality, neither position has any valid basis in the economic theory of the division of functions.

Economists divide into those who hold a normative view of central governments and those who take a more 'public choice' view. They have very different perspectives. The standard textbook assessment of the removal of trade barriers, say in Europe, concentrates on the distortions likely to ensue from non-harmonised national tax and regulatory régimes. From the formal theory of optimal taxation comes the principle that national governments within the common market should not impose significantly different taxes because supply and demand in open economies are price elastic and there would be considerable price distortions. It therefore seems appropriate that central authorities in Brussels should levy taxes.

But centralisation and harmonisation are alleged to be desirable because they make it harder for taxpayers and regulated agents to avoid the displeasure of bearing the burden, by shifting their purchases, their savings and their persons to more clement juris-dictions. By contrast, easy-to-switch activities in national economies can escape taxation. So decentralised régimes allegedly induce economic distortions, because in their attempt to avoid unfavourable tax and regulatory treatments, residents can shift their resources to less heavily taxed jurisdictions. With the removal of trade barriers, co-ordination between member-states is required. In post-1992 Europe, mobile members of the labour force will be able to avoid residence taxes, owners of capital can evade investment taxes and consumers can escape domestic VAT by buying foreign products. Strong downward pressures will be exerted on national VAT rates in Europe. In the orthodox, conventional perspective such consequences are undesirable.

Harmonisation Reduces Competition

Harmonisation is defined as convergence towards similar tax structures, similar expenditure programmes, and identical regulatory rules. Efficiency, in that framework, is seen as synonymous with maximum government revenue. It is explicit in a recent paper, which states flatly that

'the objective of each government is taken to be the maximisation of its tax revenue; all subsequent references to optimality and Pareto-efficiency are to be interpreted in that sense'.[14]

However, taking a more realistic view of governments as redistributors (rather than producers) of wealth, the overlapping of functions between levels of governments and its complement, harmonisation, are to be avoided because they serve as excuses for suppressing tax competition and for intruding into decentralised responsibilities by the central authority. By contrast, a country that dares to encroach on the jurisdiction of the common-market central authority enhances competition among governments. As the burden of such initiatives falls on the local population in an open national economy, local initiatives have the best chance of meeting real preferences. If not, they are likely to be temporary.

On the other hand, central setting of priorities and goals for (say) national environment policies or co-ordination of national agricultural marketing boards of member-states, do away with competition by removing any advantage the population might have of moving to another region or of seeking a cheaper supply in a neighbouring country. One recent measure, considered a milestone, was agreed upon by European Community finance ministers: it provides for fixing a *minimum*, not a maximum, standard rate of value-added tax of 15 per cent across the Community. In another example of 'harmonising' member-states' provisions, the European Parliament is contemplating a ban on a Swedish tradition as a condition of its entry into the common market, namely the consumption of oral snuff. Nothing short of a special dispensation will save this harmless national heritage, as well as the Danish non-conforming red sausage or Spain's carrot marmalade.

In fact, policy harmonisation does not require centrally co-ordinated action. When it serves the national interests of member-states, harmonisation between programmes, taxes and regulations occurs spontaneously through competitive market

---

14 R. Kanbur and M. Keen, *Jeux sans frontières: Tax Competition and Tax Coordination When Countries Differ in Size*, Discussion Paper No. 819, Kingston, Canada: Queen's University, May 1991, p. 8.

pressures arising from the inter-regional mobility of resources. Through the invisible hand of inter-government competition, national levels of taxation and regulations tend to converge across the common market, especially those affecting capital, the most mobile factor. Harmonisation is thus deplorable or desirable depending on whether it is imposed from the top by centralisation or whether it proceeds from decentralised choices. The first version cartelises member-states, the second expresses freedom and competition. Duplication of a central government function by a national or local authority may prove beneficial; duplication of a regional function by the central authority threatens competition and is detrimental. Central co-ordinating mechanisms have nothing to do with true federalism. They are harmful inasmuch as they are used to legitimise the cartelisation of member-states and to strengthen centralist tendencies.

The institutionalised participation of national or local regions in central policy determination on matters of common public goods should not, of course, be condemned in a democratic system. It may well be one desirable element in the complex central decision-making process. But decision-making in this arrangement remains central in nature and as such goes against the federalist logic. Whether tax, budgetary or regulatory standardisation results solely from the central parliament, or from the interaction of central and national authorities, it still suppresses competition among governments as long as it applies uniformly to the entire common market. Harmonisation arrangements belong to the central voice process rather than the exit mechanism.

Centralisation and International Income Disparities

Not only does centralisation breed inefficiency, but as a mechanism to redistribute wealth between countries and regions, it also has tragic long-term effects. Common-market policies which transfer wealth among countries reduce the concern that national economic agents would otherwise have to make necessary adjustments. In redistributionist systems, consumers and producers are discouraged from settling in those areas where their productivity is highest, because they are able, without moving, to take advantage of the hand-outs granted them by the central authority. Even though national prices are dissociated from their costs, resources need not move from regions where they are less productive. As this failure

[53]

endures, the process of income growth is hindered in less prosperous regions. Far from doing away with national disparities, policies with strong regional effects amplify them, by discouraging resources from moving to their most productive locations.

Redistributive policies of central governments foster resistance to necessary national adjustments in another way. By releasing member-countries from the consequences of their decisions, central subsidies and regulations encourage member-governments to show little concern for adopting adjustment policies themselves. Equalisation payments, cost-sharing arrangements and central regulatory measures mostly serve to shield decentralised administrations from the consequences of their bad policies. The more inefficient they are, the more they are compensated by the central authority. Over time the local economy lags further behind.

This formulation conflicts with the conventional vision of Europe as a grouping of nations associated in the task of sharing the common wealth. The political society is not a family. The instinct of man that political constitutions are supposed to contain is self-interest as defined by Hobbes.[15] Constitutions are not intended to promote altruism, but rather to exploit the self-interest motive for the benefit of the community. No political system can base its stability on altruism and no society has ever succeeded in doing so. Not all humans are equally driven by the desire for personal gain. But when the exercise of political power is involved, those people most governed by that desire are the ones most likely to become influential and dangerous. Political and constitutional organisations must be designed to contain such people and not to accommodate altruism. That altruism was not the decisive force behind the European federation or any federal state is implicit in the proposition that there is no transfer of wealth that a unitary government could not do better than a federation. In turn, this statement is based on the principle that only the holder of monopoly power can systematically transfer wealth between individuals and regions against their will. And the government of a unitary state has even more power than the central government of a federal community.

---

15 Thomas Hobbes, *Leviathan*, ed. Michael Oakeshott, Oxford: Basil Blackwell, 1986, and New York: Collier, 1986.

Harmony *vs.* Harmonisation

The idea that central assistance to lagging member economies makes for wider inequalities over the long term and slows down the necessary adjustments also helps rebut another commonly-held view. According to collectivist political orthodoxy, inter-regional transfer policies are a key element in safeguarding the unity of the whole. By redistributing wealth between nations, the parts are allegedly cemented together. The higher the disparities, the more the central government engages in lavish favours to national and local groups.

The opposing view is that central redistribution pits national groups against one another. Redistribution is less likely to bring European countries closer together than to encourage acrimony and antagonisms in taking from national communities the fruits of their efforts or their good fortune and transferring it to their neighbours, based on arbitrary formulae. Can peace, social cohesion and unity prosper as a result of standardisation and regulation at the common-market scale? Granted that regional disparities are magnified by transfers in a less flexible economy, it is clear that the whole common-market community would be less threatened by centrifugal forces, if the central authority refrained from redistributionist ambitions.

Proof that redistribution by the central power can sow the seeds of division rather than unity is supplied by the battle of the balance sheets waged in the media in relation to EC budgets. Political and journalistic accountants are already at work, tallying the balance of gains and losses obtained by each member from the central treasury. The entire exercise is analytically pointless since true federalism is not intended as a mechanism to grant favours. To attempt to determine who gains and who loses from federalism is to raise a false question, for it is not federalism's goal to redistribute wealth. As a competitive mechanism for expressing preferences for public goods, its action makes everyone a winner. It is not a *zero-sum game**. That the battle of the balance sheets has led to political marketing successes in Europe, most notably in Ireland in the summer of 1992, and in most federal states, shows that federalism has been distorted. What was initially devised as an arrangement to promote the general welfare has become the ultimate instrument for lavishing favours and privileges.

Given the inevitable tendency for central governments to usurp powers and suppress inter-governmental competition, it follows that, in contrast with the conventional wisdom, the unity of a federation does not require a strong central government. Quite the opposite is true. Ironically, academics and politicians in Europe who defend the federal idea are often those who deny the federalist principle by fighting for centralisation and convergence towards the unitary state. Such people are inconsistent and they provide weapons to extremists of the opposite camp for whom decentralisation means separation, balkanisation, and national protectionism. Centralisation is the enemy of harmony between national communities in Europe, whether they be linguistic, ethnic, religious or simply historic.

To critics who view decentralised arrangements as unstable, as an awkward half-way house between a collection of independent states and a truly unitary state,[16] the collapsing centralist régimes in Eastern Europe and in the former Soviet Union serve as a reminder that wealth redistribution by a central authority does not bring national or ethnic communities closer together. On a smaller scale, current threats to national unity in Canada are evidence that antagonisms, rather than peace and social cohesion, are likely to result from attempts by central authorities to engage in redistributive operations between regions and communities. It is unlikely that the political integration of East and West Germany has yielded more advantages than they would have enjoyed as two distinct market-oriented economies with free movement of goods and factors. Subsidising continued inefficient uses of labour and capital in the eastern part is causing more conflicts than promoting national reconciliation. Whether in Turkey, Canada, Yugoslavia, the USSR or in Europe as a whole, freedom and decentralisation appear to be a major instrument to tame ethnic feuds. When minorities have more local autonomy within loose federations and more freedom of movement across borders, they are less likely to feel oppressed and harbour hostilities. In effect, they are more likely to assimilate freely into the larger wholes in the long run. Moreover, under free-trade régimes, large-scale migrations are made less necessary and less probable by movements of capital and goods.

---

[16] This point of view is expressed in W. H. Riker, *The Development of American Federalism*, Boston: Kluwer Academic Publishers, 1987.

V. TRADE BARRIERS AND THE SIZE OF
THE PUBLIC ECONOMY: EMPIRICAL EVIDENCE

Ideally, the thesis of this paper about the causal connection between movements in trade barriers and the degree of intervention in domestic matters should be grounded on solid empirical evidence. However, there is surprisingly little factual analysis of this relationship in the economic literature. This section does not offer a systematic research programme to remedy this deficiency. Instead it uses a more humble analysis to demonstrate that the hypothesis is not inconsistent with the known facts of history.

First, it was shown in Section II that, when left free to move regionally, resources do respond to incentives, to taxes paid, to services received and to regulations applied. Economic forces at work after barriers are removed operate in the predicted fashion.

Second, an interpretation is offered of the uneasiness with which the prospect of declining trade barriers is greeted by interventionist circles in various countries. But the focus of this factual section is more on long-term trends in the level of trade barriers and their observed impact on the behaviour of national governments. The following pages concentrate on the impact of trade liberalisation within trade blocs in North America, in Europe and in other emerging freer trade zones in Asia and Latin America. National barriers between member-states no doubt remain. It is merely argued that, compared with past history, they have been immensely reduced. The North American Free Trade Area is a case in point. Instances of countervailing duties and anti-dumping regulations have been exaggerated in political circles and in the media. The truth is that relative to the level of freely-moving trade between the three partners, barriers are now negligible (magnesium, corn, Honda cars, softwood and wooden roof tiles are the most discussed). They affect less than 5 per cent of trade between Canada and the United States. The rest is free of any dispute.

Pressure Groups and Attitude toward Freer Trade

An indirect test of the analytical framework developed above is provided by the attitude of various groups towards the idea of

[57]

freer trade. Who should be the supporters and opponents of free trade in countries that consider joining neighbours in freer-trade arrangements? In the debate that preceded the free-trade pact with the United States, the battle lines were most clearly drawn in Canada, in view of the magnitude of the foreseeable changes. In addition to some producers in the most protected industries, the collection of opponents to the accord included representatives of the peace movement, environmentalists, unionists, members of the 'cultural' industries, spokesmen for the large churches and nationalists of all stripes. They were united by one common trait: their membership in the most politicised segments of the Canadian society which are also the most heavily subsidised and protected by governments in Canada. Likewise, opponents of the idea of joining the European Community in Sweden were composed of similar groupings. They used similar tactics and raised the same scare stories to put voters off in the national election of 1991.

This is no accident. On the eve of establishing perhaps the most far-reaching agreements ever on trade between neighbours, the proposed treaties could not fail to upset elements which feared for their privileged positions in their respective societies. Anti-Europe movements in Sweden claimed that, once inside the Community, social and regional programmes would have to be dismantled. Characteristically, the most ardent defenders of protectionist legislation were also the most vocal partisans of more activist 'stabilisation' policies, of expanded industrial strategies and, in general, of increased government involvement in the economy. Implicit in their view was the Rousseauist vision of government as the faithful embodiment of some abstract collective will of the national community.

Public choice analysis suggests a more illuminating statement of the impact of free trade on political decisions. A free-trade agreement, within federal unions or between sovereign states, curtails the ability of governments to spread special favours around against the will of the people, while enhancing the incentives to make efficient decisions. That is ironic for it helps expose the real goals of nationalists and opponents of free trade. What these self-appointed spokesmen of political independence are out to defend is really the further politicisation of society and the power of governments to safeguard their privileged positions.

Long-Term Trends in Trade Barriers and
Size of the Public Economy

Broad historical trends support the hypothesis that the share of
the government sector in the national economy is positively
associated with the level of trade barriers. Until the 1930s
(mostly under the old Gold Standard) there were few restrictions
on the movement of people and capital in the industrial world.
Money and goods moved in relatively large volumes. It has
taken some 70 years[1] for merchandise trade as a proportion of
GNP to overtake the levels it had achieved before the First
World War. Few quantitative barriers to trade were raised and
few obstacles impeded capital flows. Non-tariff barriers are of
comparatively recent origin and were then practically unknown.
Some Western industrial economies, including Great Britain, had
low or non-existent tariffs.

On the other hand, data now available on the long-term trend
in government expenditures in four Western countries show the
following.[2] In all four countries a sharp change of régime
occurred sometime around 1930 (at least a decade earlier in the
UK). The size of the central government in percentage of GNP
remained practically constant at 10-15 per cent over the whole
industrial era prior to this period. And then it grew sharply and
consistently until at least very recent periods. This close
relationship between the two trends in levels of protectionism
and government expenditures is not coincidental. The turning
point coincided with the onslaught of protectionism in the 1930s.
This is consistent with the thesis that spending and regulatory
instruments can be more easily employed on a large scale when
trade barriers are steep.

Some economists detect a reversal of the trend in the growth
of government expenditures and taxes in major industrial
countries.[3] Outlays seem to have peaked in the early 1980s,
sometimes earlier. Tax rates are declining in most industrialised
countries. More importantly, many governments followed the
US example in lowering their highest marginal tax rates on

---

[1] The bulk of the movement occurred between 1950 and 1970.

[2] Gordon Tullock, *Government Growth*, University of Arizona Press, March 1990 (mimeo).
The four countries are the USA, the UK, Denmark and Sweden.

[3] Richard B. McKenzie, *The Twilight of Government Growth in a Competitive World Economy*,
Cato Institute Policy Analysis No. 111, 19 August 1988; also R. B. McKenzie with
Dwight R. Lee, *Quicksilver Capital*, New York: The Free Press, 1991, mostly chapter 6,
pp. 113-57.

income.[4] Two other taxation trends, well documented in Canada and presumably observed elsewhere, underlie the competitive forces at work in more open economies in the last 30 years. They are the rise in the taxation of wages relative to capital and the lightening of the tax burden on savings relative to consumption.[5] Dampening tax-induced disincentives to save and to grow is what one would expect from lower trade barriers and the incident competition from abroad. The world-wide movement towards deregulation and privatisation in the late 1970s and 1980s is consistent with the increasing mobility of resources coincident with reduced trade barriers.

What is remarkable in these statistics is that the start of the new trend follows five rounds of successful multilateral negotiations under GATT and the advent of the European Community. In the meantime, Canada, the USA and Mexico are negotiating a free-trade agreement, as are the members of the Mercosur group, Argentina, Brazil, Paraguay and Uruguay. Similar trends in other regional blocs are observed as protectionism gives way to more formal commitments to lower barriers within a Japanese-led group in Asia and Mexican-led groups in Central and North America. The five countries[6] of the Andean Pact (1960) have also relaunched their plans for economic integration. In the same vein Eastern Europe can be viewed as moving towards a free enterprise zone. Instead of a small part of a country being freed, entire countries are being freed from constraints, while little central power appears to be in demand.

Little effort has been devoted so far to assessing methodically the relationship between protectionism and domestic interventionism. While numerous studies have been undertaken to analyse the determinants of trade barriers, on the one hand, and the size of the public economy, on the other, few analysts have attempted to relate the two phenomena. One study that comes closest to tackling these kinds of questions is a 1984 empirical study by Conybeare.[7] He finds that tariff rates in various countries are positively correlated with the size of the

[4] R. B. McKenzie and D. R. Lee, *ibid.*, pp. 117-25.

[5] For an overview of this movement in Canada, see Gérard Bélanger, 'Évolution de la taxation au Canada', *L'Analyste*, Vol. 35, Fall 1991, pp. 47-49.

[6] Peru, Bolivia, Ecuador, Colombia and Venezuela.

[7] John A. C. Conybeare, 'Tariff Protection in Developed and Developing Countries: A Cross-sectional and Longitudinal Analysis', *International Organization*, Vol. 37, 1983, pp. 441-67.

central government as a percentage of total government. This striking result is all the more significant, since another economist[8] confirms that the expansion of the public economy across countries between 1960 and 1975 is largest in unitary, highly centralised nations. In conclusion to a rich empirical debate on the relation between decentralisation and government size, a recent study shows that fiscal decentralisation is significantly associated with a smaller public sector.[9] Decentralisation at the national level tends to dampen the expansion of the public sector.

These are clearly rough estimates of the relationship between trade barriers and size of the public sector. Non-tariff barriers are not incorporated here, and the extent of interventionism is limited to the budgetary dimension, with the whole package of national regulations left out. A great deal of empirical work remains to be done before the picture becomes clear. Nevertheless, it is reassuring that casual empiricism of the kind used above is not inconsistent with the theoretical predictions, but, on the whole, is supportive of them.

[8] David R. Cameron, 'The Expansion of the Public Economy: A Comparative Analysis', *The American Political Science Review*, Vol. 72, December 1978, pp. 1,243-61.

[9] M. L. Marlow, 'Fiscal Decentralization and Government Size', *Public Choice*, Vol. 56, March 1988, pp. 259-70.

VI. CONSTITUTIONAL PRINCIPLES

This *Hobart Paper*, which is principally theoretical, cannot pretend to define a blueprint for governmental structures in emerging blocs. However, it can offer some constitutional principles which follow from its overview of federalist dynamics, and comment particularly on their application to the nascent freer-trade arrangements now being implemented in parts of the five continents, particularly in Europe.

Renewing the Constitutions of Emerging Federations

While free-trade areas and the strengthening of world competition may help to straighten the distorted governmental systems of the developed world, renewal of the structure of emerging federations by constitutional means is an opportunity not to be ignored, especially since freedom of inter-regional movement of resources (the essential condition for the proper functioning of competitive federalism) is generally not as complete between members of common-market areas as between provinces and regions of federal states. While this is less true within the EC, there are still serious obstacles to the full mobility of people, namely severe legal restrictions maintained on the movement of labour between nations. Despite the remaining impediments to the movement of goods by various quality, health and other political controls, the movement of goods and services and also of capital have been greatly liberalised in major emerging blocs; but movement of people is still far from totally free.

An important principle in revamping the system is to avoid the rigidity and obsolescence risks inherent in confining national decentralised authorities to allegedly permanent functions. As explained in the discussion on policy harmonisation (above, Section IV, pp. 50-53), economists have formal normative criteria for determining whether an activity belongs to central, national, regional, or local government. These criteria relate mainly to the presence or absence of scale economies and spillover effects of a public activity on the residents of other jurisdictions in the common-market territory. To illustrate, it is hard to envisage a province or an urban community offering defence services or the European authority controlling traffic in Berlin.

Such a technocratic view of the division of powers is, however, unhelpful. Joint supply and externalities *per se* do not justify government control unless government failures are less costly than market failures. The proper division of powers is no easier to determine than the extent of scale economies and spillover effects themselves. Neat assignment of responsibilities is impossible. The validity of a specific division is only temporary and will not withstand changes in supply and in demand conditions. For example, though the railway system and the post office may once have produced under joint-supply conditions and consequently justified some form of central political control, to-day's technology has increased the number of substitutes, making current regulations superfluous.

A fatal weakness is to base analysis on a can-do-no-wrong view of government in general, and of central authorities in particular, which leaves unaddressed the problem of state monopoly and the attraction of centralism. A systematic bias in favour of more central power follows from the textbook depiction of central government, national or supra-national, as entities only concerned with pursuing the common good. 'Benevolent despot' is the designation coined by public choice analysts to refer to this platonic view of governments as righters of market wrongs. Once a central authority is perceived to embody the collective will, it is impossible to imagine a federal structure as superior to unitary régimes. No analytical basis then stands in the way of entrusting central administrations with the task of supplying all public services, local, national and supra-national. Purely administrative decentralisation then suffices to satisfy the requirements of scale economies.[1]

---

[1] The following assessment remains the most cogent statement of the question: 'There would seem to be no reason why strictly localised public goods should not be provided by supralocal units, which might, of course, decentralise administratively as the relevant externality limits dictate. . . . There is no analysis that demonstrates the superiority of a genuinely federal political structure over a unitary structure, with the latter administratively decentralised. This result is not, in itself, surprising when we recognise that the 'economic theory' of federalism is not different from standard normative economics in its implicit assumptions about politics. The normative advice proffered by the theory is presumably directed toward the benevolent despotism that will implement the efficiency criteria. No support can be generated for a politically divided governmental structure until the prospects for nonidealised despotism are acknowledged. Once government comes to be modeled either as a complex interaction process akin to that analysed in standard public choice or, as in this book, in terms of Leviathan-like behavior, an argument for a genuinely federal structure can be developed.' (H. G. Brennan and J. M. Buchanan, *The Power to Tax: Analytical Foundations of a Fiscal Constitution*, Cambridge and New York: Cambridge University Press, 1980, pp. 174-75.)

The reality in federal states is entirely different. It offers the spectacle of uncontrollable expansion in the effective powers and intervention fields of central government, without any change in the wording of national constitutions. Conventional discussions on the virtues of European federalism in particular are mostly couched in terms of reinforcing the powers of Brussels. One can only hope (rather than expect) that the still dominant technocratic vision of governmental structures in Europe will be overcome both in the emerging common markets of Europe and North America and in the collapsing centralist régimes in the East.

Centralist Forces and the Constitutional Dilemma

The redistributionist tendencies associated with centralisation and the cartelisation of member-states, appear irresistible within a constitutional framework that gives the central government the slightest general function, such as the power to spend in the general interest or that of legislating for peace and public order, or any form of residual power such as safeguarding the economic common market.[2] The elimination of competition under central monopoly has so much appeal to privilege seekers that the collective benefits of competitive federalism apparently would not compensate. Protection against centralising forces calls for constitutional provisions of the strictest nature. Thus we are faced with a dilemma. How can the requirements of constitutional flexibility be reconciled with the necessity of protecting emerging structures from the no less constant and pressing threat of monopolisation by central government? There is no division of functions that is sufficiently watertight to satisfy this requirement completely. Yet it is important to contain the centralist threat constitutionally.

Consistent with the analysis in this paper, three constitutional federalist principles can be defined as first steps towards resolving this dilemma. To achieve the advantages of true federalism as the institutionalisation of competition between governments, it is of little use (even counterproductive) to impose restrictions on the powers of decentralised administrations and national governments of member-states in a common market. Under free trade, the instruments at the

---

[2] The general spending power provision in the Canadian constitution and the interstate commerce clause provision in the US constitution have served as entry points for the general encroachment on local jurisdictions by the central authority.

disposal of individuals to discipline national, provincial and local governments are not primarily legal and constitutional. The exit mechanism inherent in the mobility of goods and factors in a common-market area serves this purpose adequately. The only restriction on national autonomy implicit in the federalist view of the common-market governmental structure is a prohibition on member-states from interfering with the flow of goods and factors from the rest of the world, or at least from other member-states. It is mainly through their power to impose tariffs or quotas and to subsidise national producers that national governments are able to distort the rules of competitive federalism. Therefore, transferring to decentralised jurisdictions[3] the power to limit the openness of their local economy is inconsistent with the federalist ideal. In short, the constitution must guarantee the free movement of goods and factors. Apart from this major restriction, federalism appears consistent with the retention by decentralised administrations of almost all the characteristics of sovereignty. Because of the high cost they would impose on nationals, most powers of a redistributionist nature, such as monopoly education or regional development, would likely not be used under free trade.

On the other hand, the danger of central monopolisation implies imposing the firmest legal limits on the latitude of the central power. For lack of an exit process, citizens must mainly rely on the constitution to discipline the central authority. Strict checks on central powers should be included in any constitutional contract which defines the central structure. The central authority should be confined to the exercise of a small number of limited tasks where national spillover effects are so clear that they often already require national governments to enter into agreements and treaties with foreign countries. Dimensions of defence, of external affairs, of justice and police, and of trade with the outside world, are spheres which could properly be assigned to the central authority. The principle should be safeguarded that powers belong to member-states, except for those (few in number) which would be specifically assigned to the central authority. In contrast to the current European agreement, the constitution, not the Brussels authority, should have the power to make the 'subsidiarity' principle operational. As made clear in our third principle below, trade with the

---

[3] Decentralised authorities refer, it will be recalled, to governments which have no power to rule over the entire common market.

outside world would be the only area of intervention left exclusively to the central government.

In the view of several analysts, even such strict assignment rules are insufficient to confine a central structure to its defined rôle. Writers in the constitutionalist tradition argue their case from the lessons of the history of national federal structures. From their standpoint, to characterise as federal the over-centralised governmental structure of Canada, the United States, Germany, India and Australia, let alone of the former Soviet Union and Yugoslavia, shows more concern for the legal than the analytical meaning of words. As regards the emerging European structure, weak existing limitations on the powers of the European Commission, as well as the minimal effective protection of member-states' rights and citizens' rights provided by the Treaty of Rome, are seen by writers in the federalist tradition as affording still less protection from centralism.[4]

Right of Veto and Opt Out

To many constitutionalists, clear demarcation of a reduced sphere for European central bodies does not afford sufficient safeguards. Decision rules tilted in favour of national govern-ments should become part of the Community treaties. Two such rules include the right of veto by member-states, and the right for a member-state in a minority to opt out of collective decisions.[5] Some are still more pessimistic on the ability of constitutional assignment to contain the accretion of power by the community acting collectively. J. M. Buchanan, a respected authority on constitutional matters, argues that

'there must also be some explicit acknowledgement, in the contract of establishment, of the rights of citizens in the separate units to secede from union'.[6]

European institutions are in a formative stage. To outside observers the extent of effective centralisation in Europe is still a matter of debate. The Maastricht agreement is written in vague terms, open to many interpretations. Some argue it provides the

4 Frank Vibert, 'Europe's Constitutional Deficit', in *Europe's Constitutional Future*, IEA Readings No. 33, London: Institute of Economic Affairs, 1990, pp. 69-96.

5 On this issue see Frank Vibert, 'The New Europe: Constitutionalist or Centralist?', in *Europe's Constitutional Future, op. cit.*, p. 131.

6 J. M. Buchanan, 'Europe's Constitutional Opportunity', in *Europe's Constitutional Future, op. cit.*, p. 7.

legal basis for narrowing economic differences between nations through redistribution, for embarking on infrastructure projects, and for regulating centrally the social and economic conditions of production. A centralist-leaning newspaper columnist argues that 'the central institutions of the European Community have far more power than the Quebec Liberals would leave Ottawa'.[7] Yet another observer, who belongs to a generally constitutionalist newspaper, opines that, notwithstanding the formal organisational structure in place, and 'despite the mush about unity and co-operation, the EC's real purpose is to manage European national rivalries . . .', and that 'the main tactic of unification, and of EC decision in general, is the fudge'.[8] The Danish and French referenda on Maastricht have shown that the Delors vision is encountering popular resistance. The hope remains that free-market processes and institutions can still be incorporated into Europe's constitutional future.[9]

The promise of a real federalist future appears to require an active overhauling of present constitutional arrangements, not the simple straightening out of present trends. 'Subsidiarity', the principle that Brussels technocrats should handle only those tasks that national governments cannot assume, becomes an empty concept once the European Commission can decide what should and should not be locally handled. There is a danger that, through the subsidiarity principle, Europe will repeat the constitutional history of national federations like Canada and the United States. Federalism in those countries has been transformed through a series of precedents and court decisions from meaning 'constitutional decentralisation' to meaning 'contingent decentralisation', with the presumption that Congress would decide the proper division of powers.[10]

Power-Sharing

A third constitutional federalist principle would provide that, except in regard to trade with the outside world, the central authority only retains powers shared with national and other

---

[7] Jeffrey Simpson, *The Globe and Mail*, Toronto, 30 January 1991.

[8] David Brooks, 'A European Superstate? Forget it', *Wall Street Journal*, 12 August 1991.

[9] To some optimists, hope rests in the loss of 'the naïve faith in collectivist nostrums that characterised both intellectual and public attitudes for most of the 19th and 20th centuries'. (J. M. Buchanan, 'An American Perspective on Europe's Constitutional Opportunity', *The Cato Journal*, Vol. 10, Winter 1991, p. 628.)

[10] An idea developed by P. H. Aranson, 'Federalism: The Reasons of Rules', *The Cato Journal*, Vol. 10, Spring/Summer 1990, pp. 17-38.

regional administrations. Presumably, some of these powers would seldom be exercised by member-states, because of the increased burden they would imply for their residents. Nevertheless, occasional incursions of national authorities into activities of common interest and responsibility can serve as a further competitive protection against monolithic tendencies of the central administration.

Not all the functions likely to result in some international spillover effects have been identified in this paper. Certain dimensions of the environment and of other publicly-supplied services extend beyond national borders. However, alternative mechanisms exist to achieve harmonisation, less open to the centralist threat, such as agreements among national governments or delegation of authority to a central administration. Possibilities for co-operation on a flexible basis between member-states are limitless. As a case in point, the United States, Canada, Australia and Germany are parties to an agreement to co-operate in enforcing anti-trust laws. The Free Trade Agreement between Canada and the United States provides for enforcement mechanisms which constitute truly federalist processes while retaining the opting-out resort.

If the virtues of federalism are to be safeguarded, it is important that the power occasionally conceded to central authorities always follows from members delegating their constitutional powers. They must retain the freedom to withdraw such delegation at their convenience or according to the terms of the agreement. The mechanism is undoubtedly imperfect in that it involves transactions costs which may sometimes result in free rides by some members. This possible outcome merely shows that nothing is perfect. As a cost of providing citizens with a choice of government services, some residual interjurisdictional spillovers are optimal. Because integration by centralisation has its imperfections, which lie in the danger of government monopolisation, a bias should be imparted in favour of decentralisation when federations are constructed.

VII. CONCLUSION

The major force behind integration in North America, in Europe and in emerging regional blocs in Latin America and Asia is the conviction—vague but nevertheless powerful—that federalism is a good thing. The combination of a single market with decentralised national governments can work for the general welfare, because it is based on competitive principles. Competition in federalist structures flows not from uniformity but from diversity among industries and communities. At the same time, the trend towards greater freedom of resources from the confines of arbitrary national boundaries cannot fail to weaken the power of regional and national governments. The virtue of free trade is to transfer control over wealth from governments to individuals. This paper argues that a smaller share of resources will be transferred to governments under free trade; implicit in that logic is the view that those resources assigned to political allocation will conform more closely to efficiency principles.

True federalism coincident with free trade should contribute in a lasting way to the fulfilment of mankind's goal of world peace and friendship, and to the realisation of local aspirations to cultural and social development. That this message of hope and freedom coincides with Hayek's vision offered 50 years ago, is not surprising:

> 'The principle of federation is the only form of association of different peoples which will create an international order without putting an undue strain on their legitimate desire for independence.'[1]

While Hayek at the time viewed federalism as the application to international affairs of democracy with limited powers, the teachings of Tiebout, Buchanan and Hirschman have since widened its meaning. Exit under free trade, rather than voice under democratic public choice, underpins the contribution of federalism to the greater freedom of individuals.

This favourable outcome should follow from two consequences of free trade—the increase in wealth and the inability of central

---

[1] F. A. Hayek, *The Road to Serfdom*, Chicago: University of Chicago Press, 1944, p. 233.

governments to indulge in transfer activities with other people's money. Rather than pinning their hopes for improving their lot on courting the favours of a central authority, national and regional communities everywhere will then count more on creating wealth by productive effort and trade. Once the monopolistic power of the central authority is adequately contained, organised interest groups will realise that investment in political action (rent-seeking) is less profitable. They will lose their influence and their purpose, for the better good of the public as a whole. In short, redistributionism will lose its appeal, because it will be more costly to pursue. Moreover, those who under centralist and planning systems have made a career of exploiting antagonisms, conflicts, envy and hate will discover that it is harder to ensure their success by pitting regions against one another, North against South, one ethnic group against another, trade unionists against employers, cultural communities against one another, or 'good' nationals against 'bad' foreigners.

As national communities become richer, individuals will buy in the market more of the non-public goods now supplied by governments. Should they so wish, they will be able to afford more locally produced cultural activities, more government-supplied services and more complete social security systems, assuming that such services are genuinely desired by the public. If, on the other hand, the centralised and protectionist frame-work of the past has imposed more of these public commodities than the population really wants, national governments will find it harder to bring the public to support the transfers of wealth associated with these policies.

In summary, federalism and free trade should strengthen governments' power to do good, while restricting their power to abuse citizens. The independence of nations will gain from the world federalist order, because the independence of individuals will gain therefrom. In the final analysis, that is the only sovereignty which counts.

GLOSSARY

Balkanisation: When the movement of goods, capital and people is impeded by implicit or explicit trade barriers between areas of the economy, the territory is said to be balkanised. In this economic sense, balkanisation is the opposite of federalism. There are degrees of balkanisation: before the common market, Europe was more balkanised than subsequently. The Canadian economy is balkanised as a result of interprovincial barriers raised by both the Canadian government and the provinces.

Centralisation: Concentration of powers into the governmental authority which has the power to tax and regulate the whole economy where trade is free. This enables the central government to dissociate local prices from local costs by regulation and uniform provision of public services. Concentration into the central government occurs behind trade barriers in traditional federal states or at the level of the central authority in common markets.

Federalism: Formally it can designate any governmental structure where the functions of the state are divided between more than one layer of government. Conventionally the term is reserved for régimes where the 'sovereign' powers of the state are constitutionally divided between the national authority and lower levels of governments such as provinces, cantons or states. The economic concept of federalism more broadly refers to any political structure where the power of political authorities extends to less than the size of the economy in which resource movement is unimpeded by trade barriers. Such régimes enhance the ability of resource owners to move their goods, their capital or themselves away from tax and regulatory measures that are detrimental to them.

Free-Riding: Some services exhibit the property that they simultaneously provide benefits to more than one individual at the same time. Some individuals may not find it rational to contribute voluntarily to the financing of such services in the belief that others in the community will contribute enough to produce them. They are then said to free-ride on their neighbours. This process is viewed by many as the foundation of the liberal theory of the state according to which the state is necessary because people will not voluntarily co-operate to provide themselves with public goods.

Negative-sum game: A phrase loosely borrowed from game theory. It is here used to describe the process of political action (rent-seeking) in which interest groups engage to obtain transfers and favours from the government. To the extent that resources are consumed for the purpose of merely transferring wealth as opposed to producing wealth, the operation implies a net loss (hence a negative sum).

Prisoner's dilemma: A game assumed to represent the public goods problem, in which each player (individuals in a community) can either co-operate or defect and receive a pay-off based on the other's choice. While the public goods tradition argues that the safest strategy is mutual defection, recent contributions show that repeated plays can lead to co-operation (voluntary contribution) instead.

Property rights: Entitlement of resource owners to the whole product of such resources. Property rights can be assigned to a closed class or to an open class of owners. In the former case, potential users of the resource services must first purchase the right to them from current owners. Rent-seeking *(q.v.)* is then ruled out. In the latter case, potential users can have access to the product of a resource without having previously purchased the right from current owners. They can simply invest in political activities to obtain a transfer through a political decision or migrate to a region better endowed in that resource. Rent-seeking is then said to take place.

Public or collective goods: Goods that all or most individuals want but for whose production people do not find it rational to contribute voluntarily in the belief that others in the community will contribute enough to produce them. Hence the free-rider problem *(q.v.)*. A characteristic of such goods is the high cost of excluding any person from enjoying them (for example, national defence). Joint supply is also typical of those goods as a result of some highly indivisible production factors: it follows that the

[72]

marginal cost is low, with the result that monopoly is said to be the most efficient industry structure (for example, the service of a bridge over a river).

Rent-seeking: Any activity engaged in for the purpose of obtaining wealth transfers, as opposed to activities devoted to increasing the production of wealth. Revenues raised by governments, the distribution of which is determined by political competition among rival interest groups, give rise to rent-seeking. Migrations of resources into territories better endowed in resources for the purpose of sharing in the product of taxes are also expressions of rent-seeking. Rent-seeking activities follow from conditions where property rights to resources are left unspecified or assigned to an open class.

Spillover effects, neighbourhood effects: Conditions where decisions made by a government result in benefits and/or costs that extend beyond the territory over which it has jurisdiction. In conventional normative economics, such a situation is said to call for centralisation or compensatory payments and/or levies by a central authority. Vesting local communities and national governments in common markets with full property rights over natural characteristics and differential rental incomes in their territory can provide the same efficiency outcome without the dangers of central monopoly. Decentralised governments have the incentives and the power to rely only on taxes and regulations that are compensated by services. Such taxes and regulations become fees for services and as such rule out spillovers.

Tiebout approach or process: A process whereby individuals voluntarily congregate into communities made up of people with similar tastes for public services. The process underlies the economic concept of federalism whereby the movement of people brings governments to supply public services whose value is at least as high as taxes to finance them. In the task of constructing a federalist world, the Tiebout process is supplemented by the mobility of other resources, namely goods and capital.

Zero-sum game: In transfers made by the government between individuals or groups, the benefits of gainers exactly cancel the losses of losers, when viewed in isolation. The game is then said to be zero-sum. To the extent that beneficiaries and victims have invested time and money to gain access to such transfers or to protect themselves from them, the game is transformed into a negative sum. The difference is accounted for by resources devoted to rent-seeking *(q.v.)*.

Federalism and Free Trade
JEAN-LUC MIGUÉ

Protectionism has become less and less of a viable instrument of intervention by national governments, particularly for member-states of common markets. This *Hobart Paper* provides a formal framework for analysing the effect on domestic policy choices of constraining the power of national governments to maintain trade barriers, as experienced in GATT-type arrangements, in common-market treaties, and in other freer-trade agreements within blocs of trading partners. The author, Professor Jean-Luc Migué of the University of Quebec, argues that the government of a national economy with free inward and outward movement of factors and goods, has little or no power to engage in purely redistributive policies. The member governments of a common market are in a position approximating that of the government of a small economy, free of trade barriers. Federalism and free trade go hand in hand inasmuch as they both strengthen governments' power to do good, while restricting their power to abuse citizens.

The paper attempts to show that the opening of national frontiers to freer movement of goods, services, capital, and people will result in less use of other instruments of intervention in domestic affairs. Less reliance on protectionism by national governments will have an impact similar to reinforcing devolution of power within federal states. Imposing heavier taxes and restrictive regulations on national resources in conditions of free trade leads first to more rapid and more pronounced substitution of foreign for local production. It also causes capital to move out of higher-cost economies. Finally, victims of government abuse may 'vote with their feet' and leave the territory. Freer trade is a first step and a sufficient condition towards the federalisation of the world.

However, this competitive federalist model only works if national and local decisions are not superseded by vast central powers covering the same fields within trade blocs or at the supra-national level. As a tool for cartelising national and regional governments, centralisation weakens the ability of citizens to escape unpopular measures by moving their goods or their production factors to more favourable locations and uses.

ISBN 0-255 36320-6

Hobart Paper 122

The Institute of Economic Affairs
2 Lord North Street, Westminster
London SW1P 3LB
Telephone: 071-799 3745

£7.95

IEA PUBLICATIONS
SUBSCRIPTION SERVICE

An annual subscription is the most convenient way to obtain our publications. Every title we produce in all our regular series will be sent to you immediately on publication and without further charge, representing a substantial saving.

Individual subscription rates* for 1993

Britain:	£30·00 p.a.
	£28·00 p.a. if paid by Banker's Order.
	£18·00 p.a. to teachers and students who pay *personally*.
Europe:	£30·00 p.a.
Rest of the world:	£40·00 p.a. Surface Mail; Airmail Rates on application.

* These rates are *not* available to companies or to institutions.

To: The Treasurer,
Institute of Economic Affairs,
2 Lord North Street,
Westminster,
LONDON SW1P 3LB

I should like to subscribe from: Month:................................

Year:.....................

[Subscription can be taken out for past years; please indicate which you would like to include.]

☐ I enclose a cheque made payable to
The Institute of Economic Affairs for £............................

☐ Please charge my Access / Barclaycard / Diners Club / American Express / Visa / Mastercard
Number............................ Expiry Date..................

NAME AND ADDRESS (Please print)

....

....

....

.... Postcode....................

Signature................................... Date........................

I am a teacher/student at ....
.... (where applicable)

HP122

TOPICS/QUESTIONS FOR DISCUSSION

1. The defining characteristic of federalism is that most public services are supplied by governments which have no power to rule over the entire territory where trade is free.

2. The Hoover Co. recently moved its vacuum cleaner installations from a city in France to a small town in Scotland to take advantage of less strict working conditions and labour regulations. An indignant Prime Minister of France coined the expression 'social dumping' to characterise the move. Discuss.

3. To what extent is exit under free trade preferable to voice under democratic public choice?

4. Free trade with limited supra-national authority in Europe places each national government in the approximate position of a province or a state or a canton within national federations.

5. The power to move their resources, not political action, is the instrument at the disposal of individuals to discipline governments in a federalist régime. Discuss.

6. Trade barriers as a policy tool stand out as fundamentally different from other instruments such as taxation, expenditure and regulation. Why?

7. Private property rights and a federalist governmental structure are two conditions essential to the working of a free and prosperous society under capitalism.

8. A full currency union à la Maastricht, combined with inter-regional fiscal transfers, would not suppress currency instability in Europe. Why not?

9. Why is the conventional goal of tax neutrality viewed as

suspicious by the defenders of individual freedom and prosperity?

10. Why is rent-seeking by inter-regional migration a consequence of the incomplete assignment of property rights in local resources?

11. A strong central government in Brussels or in any federal structure neutralises the competitive government process by making the mobility of resources inoperative.

12. Why does the centralised provision of public services from Brussels act as an implicit subsidy to consumers and producers in lagging and less conservative member-states of the common market?

13. For an effective protection against balkanisation and for a fuller European economic integration, minimal political integration should be sought.

14. Centralised monopoly power in Brussels contributes to rent-seeking by regional groups.

15. Policy harmonisation between national governments in a common market does not require centrally co-ordinated action. Harmonisation spontaneously occurs as a result of competitive pressures arising from resource mobility.

16. Far from attenuating national income disparities between member-states, central policies with strong regional effects amplify them, by discouraging resources from moving to their most productive location.

17. Did the political integration of East and West Germany bring about fewer advantages than both regions could have obtained as two distinct market-oriented economies under free trade?

18. The veto right and the right to opt out of collective decisions by member-states are two desirable rules to tilt a European constitution in favour of national authorities.

FURTHER READING

P. H. Aranson 'Federalism: The Reasons of Rules', *The Cato Journal*, Vol. 10, Spring/Summer 1990, pp. 17-38.

B. L. Benson, 'Interstate Tax Competition, Incentives to Collude, and Federal Influences', *The Cato Journal*, Vol. 10, Spring/Summer 1990, pp. 75-90.

H. G. Brennan and J. M. Buchanan, *The Power to Tax, Analytical Foundations of a Fiscal Constitution*, Cambridge and New York: Cambridge University Press, 1980.

J. M. Buchanan, 'An Economic Theory of Clubs', *Economica*, Vol. 32, February 1965, pp. 1-14.

W. A. Fischel, 'Property Taxation and the Tiebout Model: Evidence for the Benefit View from Zoning and Voting', *Journal of Economic Literature*, Vol. 30, March 1992, pp. 171-77.

R. W. Hahn, 'Instrument Choice, Political Reform and Economic Welfare', *Public Choice*, Vol. 67, December 1990, pp. 243-56.

A. O. Hirschman, *Exit, Voice and Loyalty*, Cambridge, Mass.: Harvard University Press, 1970.

A. O. Krueger, 'The Political Economy of the Rent-Seeking Society', *American Economic Review*, Vol. 64, June 1974, pp. 291-303.

M. L. Marlow, 'Fiscal Decentralization and Government Size', *Public Choice*, Vol. 56, March 1988, pp. 259-70.

J.-L. Migué, 'Trade Barriers in the Theory of Instrument Choice', *The Cato Journal*, Vol. 12, Fall/Summer 1992 (forthcoming).

C. M. Tiebout, 'A Pure Theory of Local Expenditures', *Journal of Political Economy*, Vol. 64, October 1956, pp. 416-24.

Frank Vibert, 'The New Europe: Constitutionalist or Centralist?', in *Europe's Constitutional Future*, IEA Readings No. 33, London: Institute of Economic Affairs, 1990, pp. 121-44.

TESTING THE MARKET
Competitive Tendering for Government Services in Britain and Abroad

ROBERT CARNAGHAN & BARRY BRACEWELL-MILNES

In Research Monograph 49 Robert Carnaghan and Barry Bracewell-Milnes review experience with competitive tendering for government services in Britain and abroad and make the following 10 recommendations:

1. Competitive tendering for the management of a small number of hospitals should be introduced on a trial basis, subject to appropriate safeguards.

2. The emphasis of council and health authority members should be less on the workings of the services provided by their organisations and more on the needs and problems to be met, the extent to which they are being met, and how they can be met more effectively.

3. The Audit Commission should investigate why many local authorities have contracted out very few or none of the services subject to CCT; its results and conclusions should be published.

4. Councils which do not use or propose to use in-house suppliers for a defined service are not at present affected in respect of that service by the CCT legislation. They should be required to use competitive tendering unless they can show good reason why it should not be used.

5. Local and health authorities should be obliged to divide proposed contracts which are greater in size than a set level (dependent on the activity) into separate contracts for tendering purposes. This would permit either distribution of the work between different contractors or its amalgamation, depending on which proves in practice to be more economical. Economies or diseconomies of scale should be discovered rather than assumed.

6. Consideration should be given to altering the *de minimis* figure,

---

ISBN 0-255 36317-6   Research Monograph 49   **£14·95**

THE INSTITUTE OF ECONOMIC AFFAIRS
2 Lord North Street, Westminster
London SW1P 3LB   Telephone: 071-799 3745

above which local authority work for a single activity is subject to compulsory competition.

7. Direct service organisations should be free to buy the supplies they require competitively, rather than being tied to in-house provision.

8. Authorities should be encouraged to experiment with inviting tenders for different levels of service rather than simply for a single specification. Market research should be used to discover those service levels which the public prefer when given knowledge of relative costs.

9. Competitive tendering should gradually be extended to the fire services and to suitable aspects of police work so as to test and improve their efficiency.

10. Directives from the European Community require careful scrutiny lest they become an unnecessary burden as well as being a far greater burden in practice for local authorities in Britain than for those in other countries.

The State of the Economy 1993

Every year the IEA convenes a number of eminent economic analysts to express their views about economic prospects and policy at its State of the Economy conference.

In late January 1993, at a time of great uncertainty about prospects for the British economy and about future monetary arrangements in Europe, nine eminent economists addressed the IEA Conference. The speakers, whose papers (revised where necessary) are included in this volume, were four of the 'wise men'—Professors Congdon, Currie, Godley and Minford—from the Chancellor of the Exchequer's Panel of Independent Forecasters; two very well-known economists from abroad—Sir Alan Walters, former adviser to Mrs Margaret (now Lady) Thatcher and Professor Roland Vaubel of the University of Mannheim; Professor John Muellbauer who has made a special study of the British housing market; and two of the City's most prominent forecasters, Bill Martin and Neil MacKinnon.

The papers not only assess the state of the economy but examine the outlook and provide insights into areas of agreement among economists of different persuasions (for example, on interest rate policy) as well as significant disagreements (for example, over whether taxes should be increased).

CONTENTS

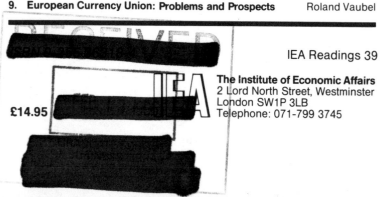

IEA Readings 39

The Institute of Economic Affairs
2 Lord North Street, Westminster
London SW1P 3LB
Telephone: 071-799 3745

£14.95